Communicating with pattern

Signs and symbols

RotoVision

Published and distributed by RotoVision SA
Route Suisse 9, CH-1295, Mies, Switzerland
RotoVision SA, Sales and Editorial Office
Sheridan House, 114 Western Road, Hove
BN3 1DD, UK
Tel: + 44 (0) 1273 72 72 68
Fax: + 44 (0) 1273 72 72 69
Email: sales@rotovision.com
Web: www.rotovision.com

10 9 8 7 6 5 4 3 2 1
ISBN 978-2-940361-90-8

Original book concept: Keith Stephenson, Luke Herriott
Art direction: Tony Seddon
Design and artwork: Keith and Spike
at Absolute Zero Degrees
Special photography: Leo Reynolds
Additional illustrations: Keith Stephenson

Reprographics in Singapore by Provision PTE.
Printed in Singapore by Star Standard Industries PTE.

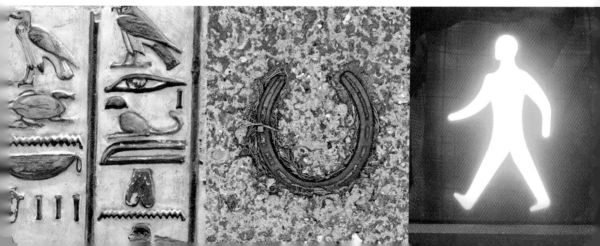

Communicating with pattern

Signs and symbols

Mark Hampshire & Keith Stephenson

Contents

Foreword

What is the first sign or symbol you remember seeing? The first one I remember is either my dad's WWII Captain's bars, or Pegasus, a big red winged horse on the side of the oil truck that brought the winter oil to my grandmother's home. I loved seeing both of them.

I asked a young designer and the first memory was the "restroom" sign. Maybe not as romantic, but certainly an indication that public services have joined the military and the commercial world as major users of signs and symbols.

I have another thought about my first memories. There are earlier experiences that were more content than studied graphic form. A smile, an open hand, a waving finger, my dog—the important stuff. It was probably similar observations that prompted humankind to find graphic ways to represent content.

Content enables communication, and form determines its degree of success. Our ancient ancestors have left us images carved into rock and painted on cave walls. They figured out how to put the world around them and meaningful human gestures into visual form. Technology has made it easier, but we are still learning how to design and use signs and symbols.

© Lance Wyman 2008

001 Earth Day New York logo designed by Lance Wyman Ltd.

Introduction

A bilingual street sign observed recently in the UK carried a warning in English reading "pedestrians look right," with a Welsh translation beneath reading "pedestrians look left:" a linguistic mistake giving conflicting directions. Little wonder that public signage attempts as much as possible to communicate without words—the use of icons and pictograms frequently offering greater clarity of information.

Signs and symbols proliferate in the modern world to the extent that it's easy to take them for granted: on directional signage, food packaging, airplane tailfins, garment care labels, and personal technology devices. Key to the discipline of graphic design, signs and symbols enable an idea, message, or theme to be summed up succinctly and compellingly. But while it's easy to think of them as cutting across language barriers, increasing understanding, and ultimately simplifying life, this is a utopian view. Because the function of signs and symbols requires that we're all interpreting them by the same set of rules. The reality is that no rulebook exists; semiotic studies reveal that the development of signs and symbols is governed by a host of historical, social, and cultural variables)

In his foreword to *The Complete Dictionary of Symbols*, Jack Tresidder asserts: "symbols read differently according to their context. For example, the dragon became a symbol of evil and disorder in the West but in the East represents the fertilizing power of thunder and rain." Different cultures adopt signs and symbols to represent life's big themes: science and religion, good and evil, life and death, love and luck all have associated symbols. Context is key to understanding why these signs have been appropriated and how they have been imbued with particular meaning. Symbols are sometimes misappropriated too: the swastika, an Eastern symbol representing good fortune and wellbeing, was hijacked by Hitler's Nazi party, demonstrating at once the power of symbols and how they can acquire entirely fabricated associations.

002 A collection of posters by designer Michael Braley, of Braley Design, to promote various lectures for the AIGA. Top left, The Design Process, featuring a rabbit being pulled from a hat. Top right and bottom left, Good Client, Bad Client. Bottom right, promotion for Michael Braley's poster design workshop at Wichita State University.

The notion of symbolism brings a nuance of meaning that goes beyond the rational communication of information. Signs and symbols are open to interpretation, which obfuscates but also intrigues, making them the focus for much conjecture and speculation, as evinced by the plethora of websites devoted to mystical signs and their supposed meanings. What is a sign to one is a puzzle to another; the Egyptian hieroglyphic system went untranslated for almost 14 centuries until the code was cracked with the discovery of the Rosetta Stone.

To date, the *Communicating with Pattern* series has been concerned with the decoding of pattern: understanding how it is used to convey specific ideas and information. The series has explored the accentuating nature of stripes, the inclusiveness of circles, and the orderliness of squares. Including signs and symbols in the series introduces a broader source of pattern and a bigger task: both to understand the general communication functions of signs and symbols, and to consider how they reflect society's values, desires, hopes, and fears. Therefore, pictogram obsessives take note: while we include many examples of instructional and directional signs, here you will not find page after page of icons. Instead, we draw on popular symbolism, myth, and legend; we feature communication design per se and also design inspired by communication; we extrapolate signs and symbols from the environment, and explore illustration that displays an icon-like appearance. Our net is cast wide to reflect the constantly changing nature of signs and symbols—evolving to meet the demands of changing behavior, beliefs, and methods of communication.

Communicating with pattern: Signs and symbols identifies in four key sections some of the most prevalent symbols in historical and modern usage. We open with a look at early signs that embody man's first attempts to communicate, commemorate events, and understand the universe. Next we explore symbols of identity and membership: representing religious belief, political alignment, and cultural and personal identity. In the next chapter we feature the vast array of themes and moods that are communicated through signs and symbols: from war and peace to science and space, sport and activity to food and drink. Finally, we examine the functional signs and symbols that convey information, taking in musical notation, wayfinding icons, sign language, and health and safety. The result is an overview of current sign and symbol usage across the creative disciplines, including art, architecture, communication design, and contemporary print and pattern.

The Design Process
Michael Bierut
Iowa State University
College of Design
Kocimski Auditorium
October 21, 2004

Michael Braley / May 25, 2006 / AIGA Kansas City

Good Client Bad Client

Good Client / Bad Client / Michael Braley / February 23, 2006 / USC McMaster Building / Columbia, South Carolina

Michael Braley
Poster Design Workshop
Wichita State University
November 11-12, 2005

Early Symbols

Petroglyphs and Cave Paintings
Hieroglyphs
The Rosetta Stone
Astronomy and Astrology
Alchemy

Early Symbols

An overview of early symbols highlights their importance to human progress, because symbols are intrinsically linked to our ability to communicate. The earliest petroglyphs might have been created as part of religious ceremonies, or formed the basis of early maps—there are many theories. They represent the start of pictorial communication that was refined by the ancient Egyptians as hieroglyphic script. Not until the discovery of the Rosetta Stone in the late 18th century were we able to decode these ancient religious writings.

Many of the signs we use today have evolved from early symbols. Astrology and astronomy share symbols for planets that were first named by the ancient Greeks, while modern chemistry arranges elements in a format that has evolved from its tenebrous predecessor, alchemy.

003 Petroglyphs at Newspaper Rock near Indian Creek, Utah, USA.
004 Signs of the Zodiac.
005 Colorful Egyptian hieroglyphs.
006 Maori cliff carving, Taupo, New Zealand. The carving has become an important cultural attraction for the region; an example of traditional Maori knowledge and skills.
007 The alchemical symbol for air.
008 Zodiac fabric.
009 The rooster is one of the 12 signs of the Chinese zodiac—depicted here through the medium of traditional Chinese paper cutting.

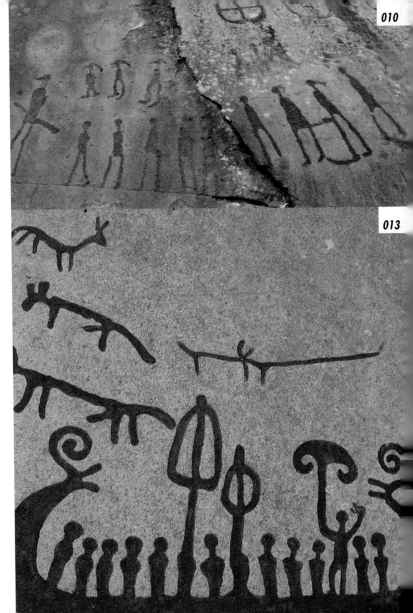

Petroglyphs and Cave Paintings

With the oldest examples dating back to the Upper Paleolithic era, petroglyphs—carvings or etchings made on rocks—and cave paintings represent the earliest examples of man communicating through signs and symbols. These visceral images, depicting an enigmatic primitive existence, hold a fascination for modern cultures everywhere.

Whether they constituted a form of symbolic communication, were used as maps and astronomical markers, or played a part in religious or magic ceremonies, one of the most puzzling things about these carvings is the similarity they bear to one another, regardless of geographical location. Decoding the images provides historians with an enormously rich insight into the life of prehistoric man, resulting in a site like the Vitlycke stone near Tanumshede in western Sweden being declared a World Heritage Site by UNESCO. Some glyphs at Tanumshede feature wagons and hunting scenes, along with images of agricultural activities, such as ploughing with oxen. Other scenes portray long boats carrying around a dozen passengers—indicating that Scandinavian Bronze and Iron Age people were already seafaring. →

010 and 013 Nordic Bronze Age petroglyphs on the Vitlycke stone, near Tanumshede, western Sweden. Despite being a UNESCO World Heritage site, the petroglyphs have been painted red to make them more visible.
011 Mongolian petroglyphs captured by Jannie Armstrong.
012 Maori cliff carving, Taupo, New Zealand.

MYSTΞRY WALK · M+M

"When it was decided that the fifth Martha and the Muffins album was to be called *Mystery Walk*, I immediately thought of the Peterborough petroglyphs [in Ontario], which I had first seen during the late 1970s—scores of strange, otherworldly figures and symbols covering a large, white outcrop of limestone. Only three of us were there amid the snowbound forest, which only increased the atmosphere of mystery and isolation.

"Obtaining permission from the Ontario Ministry of Natural Resources, I returned and took the photographs for the album cover. I designed the cover with the intention of wanting the viewer to feel as though the figures were floating, without gravity, as if they had become disengaged from time and space.

"I have the sense that the artists who made these incredible markings so many centuries ago may have wanted to convey that feeling as well."

**Mark Gane,
Martha and the Muffins**

→ Drawn with red and yellow ocher, hematite, manganese oxide, and charcoal, the earliest European cave paintings, like those at Altamira in Spain and Lascaux in France, date back 32,000 years, with other examples found in Mexico, Australia, and Africa. Since they're often found deep inside caves with no evidence of habitation, it's unlikely they were created for decorative purposes. Commonly depicting animals such as bison, deer, or horses, most theories attribute them to ritualistic ceremonies intended to help men catch the animals they hunted or as part of shamanic or religious ceremonies.

014 *The cover of "Mystery Walk" by Canadian post-punk band, Martha and the Muffins, designed by Mark Gane. The design juxtaposes ancient petroglyphs with a modern sans serif typeface, which has a runic quality.*
015 *Petroglyphs at Newspaper Rock near Indian Creek, Utah, USA, likely to have been carved by people of the Archaic, Basketmaker, Fremont, or Pueblo cultures.*
016–017 *Inspired by cave paintings? A piece of public art seen in London's Notting Hill.*

015

016

017

Hieroglyphs

Over 6,000 years ago, the ancient Egyptians invented written scripts for the purpose of recording and communicating information about political and religious affairs. At least three scripts were used for different purposes; among them, the hieroglyphic system is the most widely known today. Yet until the beginning of the 19th century these symbols had become totally inscrutable.

Meaning "sacred carvings," the first hieroglyphs were carved on buildings; later they were written on papyrus scrolls. Like all signs and symbols, hieroglyphs fall into a number of categories, which vary according to function and usage. Early hieroglyphs were simple pictures representing the words for well-known objects. Others were used symbolically: water was represented by three wavy lines, sight by an eye, and so on. Alphabetical symbols represented individual sounds or syllables to convey phonetic information. By the 9th century BC hieroglyphs had become more like handwriting, with the pictures used as letters to represent sounds and other hieroglyphs employed to help the reader understand the meaning: a sign of a sealed roll of papyrus, for instance, indicated an abstract idea. Having been limited to use by the religious leaders of Egypt, hieroglyphs became obsolete after the end of the 4th century AD and the knowledge of how to read and write them disappeared until the discovery of the Rosetta Stone provided the key to the language.

018 Hieroglyphs on the terrace of the Great Temple of Ramses II at Abu Simbel, Egypt.
019 Detail of a wall carved with hieroglyphs.
020 Painted hieroglyphs in earthy tones.

The Rosetta Stone

Soldiers in Napoleon's army uncovered this slab of inscribed granodiorite in 1799 at Rosetta in the Nile delta during the battle between the French and the Mamelukes. Following Napoleon's defeat, the stone passed into British ownership and went on display at the British Museum, giving rise to a battle of another sort: two academics, one British, one French, fought to become the first to decipher the writing on the stone.

It bears a decree from King Ptolemy V, passed by a council of priests at Memphis in 195 BC, describing the repealing of various taxes and instructions to erect statues in temples. The same passage is written in three scripts: hieroglyphs (used mainly for religious documents), demotic (the everyday native script), and Greek (used by the administration of Egypt's then Greek rulers). Thomas Young, an English physicist, was the first to show that some of the hieroglyphs wrote the sounds of a royal name, but it was a French scholar, Jean-François Champollion, who finally deciphered it in 1822.

Able to read both Greek and Coptic, Champollion worked out how the seven demotic signs were used in Coptic and traced the demotic signs back to hieroglyphic signs. He made educated guesses about what the other hieroglyphs stood for, providing the clue to the meaning of the mysterious writings on Egyptian monuments and papyrus rolls. The Rosetta Stone vastly increased our knowledge of ancient Egypt and stands today as an example of early code-cracking and a symbol of multilingualism, even giving its name to a brand of language-learning software.

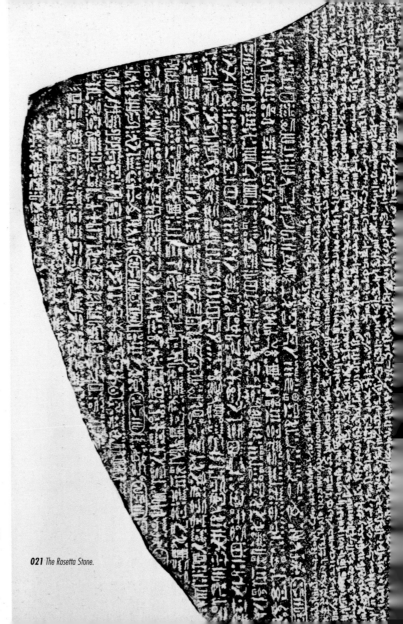

021 *The Rosetta Stone.*

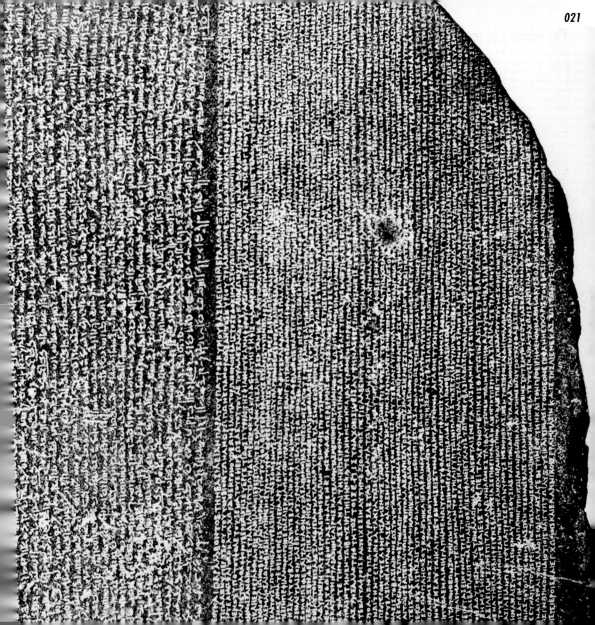

Astronomy and Astrology

Experts in astronomy, the scientific study of matter in outer space, are always keen to distance themselves from the less tangible practice of astrology, the study of the stars and their influence on people's lives. But until the invention of the telescope in the 16th century provided the key to real understanding of the universe, the two were entirely linked. The ancient Babylonians, Greeks, and Romans named the planets after their deities. Today, the same signs for the planets are used in both astrology and astronomy, emphasizing the way that the empirical science has evolved from more mystical beginnings: the planet Mars, for instance is represented by the shield and spear of the god of war; the symbol for Neptune is the trident of the sea god. Recent planet discoveries use more logical symbols—Pluto, discovered in 1930, is represented by the P and L from its name (which are also the initials of Percival Lowell, who predicted its discovery).

Modern astronomy divides the sky into 88 constellations. A constellation is a group of stars visible within a particular region of the night sky —so to say that a planet is in the constellation Aquarius helps to locate the planet on the celestial sphere. Again, astronomy owes many of these names to ancient civilizations that first identified shapes and patterns in the groups of stars to make it easier to find them among the thousands of stars in the sky. →

Sun	Mercury	Venus	Earth	Moon

Mars	Jupiter	Saturn	Uranus	Neptune	Pluto

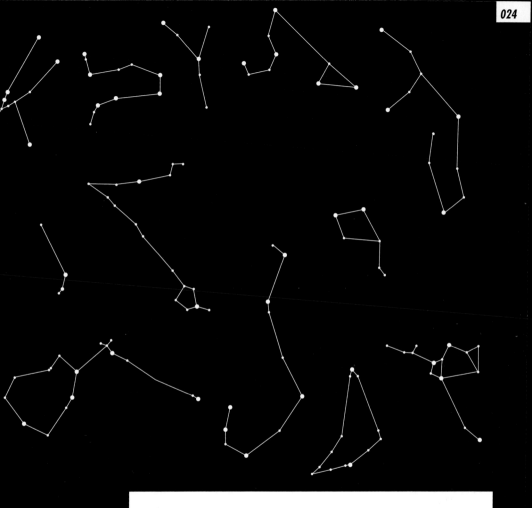

022 Constellation collection of glassware by designers, Rimmington Vian.
023 Symbols developed to represent the planets.
024 Simplified constellations of the zodiac:
(Top, L/R) Taurus, Gemini, Cancer, Leo, Virgo

(Middle, L/R) Aries, Pisces
(Middle, far right) Libra
(Bottom, L/R) Aquarius, Scorpio, Capricorn, Sagittarius

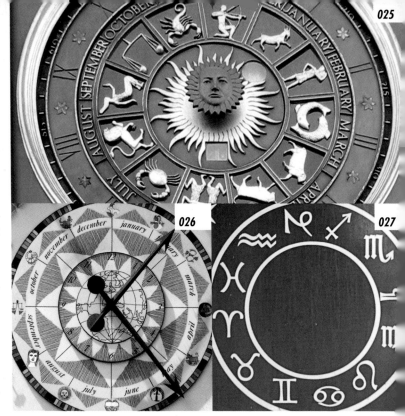

025

→ The star groups were named for animals, gods, and myths: Leo is the Latin for lion, Andromeda was a Greek mythological heroine. Between the 15th and 18th centuries European navigators named constellations in the Southern Hemisphere for scientific instruments and recently discovered animals, reflecting a more enlightened world: Telescopium after the telescope, Tucana after the toucan.

The zodiac is an imaginary band 18 degrees wide and centered on the path of the sun. Its 12 constellations are familiar to all Western followers of astrology as star signs. Divided into four elements—fire, earth, air, and water—they are believed to represent 12 basic personality types. Chinese astrology is based on the interaction of two separate cycles: the five elements of wood, fire, earth, metal, and water and the 12 zodiac animal signs of rat, ox, tiger, rabbit, dragon, snake, horse, sheep, monkey, rooster, dog, and boar. This combination of five elements and 12 animals creates the 60-year cycle, which always starts with wood rat and ends with water boar.

026

027

025 The 12 signs of the zodiac mapped out against their corresponding months.
026 Zodiac clock where the symbols are replaced with pictorial representations of the signs.
027 Panel depicting the signs of the zodiac.
028 The signs of the zodiac are often represented pictorially, as in these icons.
029 Images of artist Tchenka Jane Sunderland's Zodiac Garden, which surrounds her labyrinth, set out in Wensum Park, Norfolk, UK.
030 Simplified symbols developed to represent the 12 constellations.

028

ARIES 21·III · 20·IV ✿ RED — INITIATING & PIONEERING

TAURUS 21·IV · 21·V ✿ PINK — GROWTH & FERTILITY

GEMINI 22·V · 21·VI ✿ YELLOW — TRAVEL & COMMUNICATION

CANCER 22·VI · 23·VII ✿ WHITE — NURTURING & ENABLING

LEO 24·VII · 23·VIII ✿ ORANGE — RULERSHIP & SELF EXPRESSION

VIRGO 24·VIII · 23·IX ✿ YELLOW — HEALTH & EFFICIENCY

LIBRA 24·IX · 23·X ✿ PINK — PARTNERSHIP & BALANCE

SCORPIO 24·X · 22·XI ✿ DARK RED — DEATH & REBIRTH

SAGITTARIUS 23·XI · 21·XII ✿ PURPLE — ADVENTURE & BELIEF

CAPRICORN 22·XII · 20·I ✿ DARK BLUE — AMBITION & RESPONSIBILITY

AQUARIUS 21·I · 19·II ✿ ELECTRIC BLUE — GROUP CONSCIOUSNESS

PISCES 20·II · 20·III ✿ PURPLE — COMPASSION & IMAGINATION

031 Paper-cut Chinese horoscope symbols—the rooster, the pig, and the rabbit.

032 Year of the Pig New Year party flyer designed by New York based designer Nicholas Felton.

033 Stylized Chinese horoscope figures, featuring from left to right: rat, ox, tiger, rabbit, dragon, snake, horse, sheep, monkey, rooster, dog, and boar.

Alchemy

The predecessors of modern chemists, alchemists experimented with the transformation of natural materials. Notoriously, they sought to turn lead into gold. Originating in the east around the 5th century BC, alchemy spread west via the medieval Islamic world, reaching its apogee in 16th- and 17th-century Europe. Dismissed today as a mystical hotchpotch of science, magic, and witchcraft practiced by charlatans greedily pursuing impossible goals, it's worth remembering that Isaac Newton wrote many manuscripts on alchemy, and the father of nuclear physics, Ernest Rutherford, called himself an alchemist. Furthermore, alchemical methods of distillation and extraction using beakers, crucibles, and filters resonate with modern laboratory practices and equipment.

Also recognizable is the system of using symbols to represent the elements. Modern science has the Periodic Table, and alchemy had its own set of symbols for each of the key elements. In the early days of alchemy, the astronomical signs of the planets were used, with specific symbols later being developed. Even then, little standardization was achieved—a reflection of the often shady and secretive practices associated with alchemy, its practitioners employing a variety of codes and symbols in a bid to conceal their findings from potential rivals.

034 Sometimes referred to as the Philosopher's Stone, the symbol for alchemy incorporporates the circle of the macro cosmos, the circle of the micro cosmos, the triangle of the three human components, and the square of the four alchemical elements.
035 Alchemical symbol for air.
036 Alchemical symbol for earth.
037 Alchemical symbol for fire.
038 Alchemical symbol for water.
039 Alchemical symbols for elements.

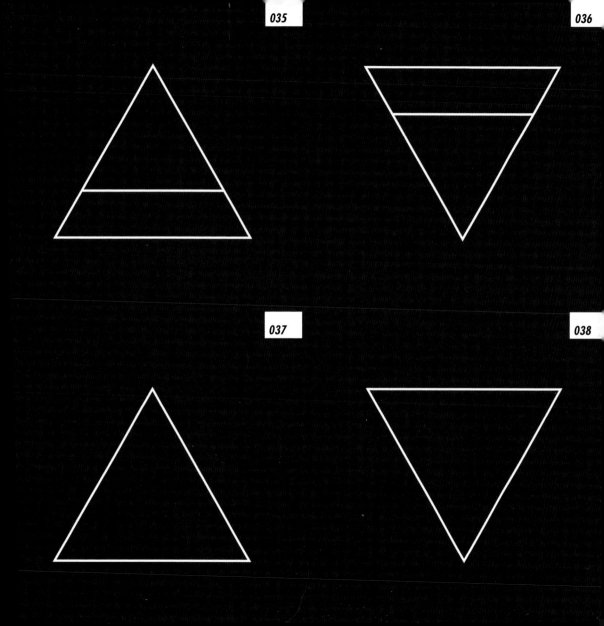

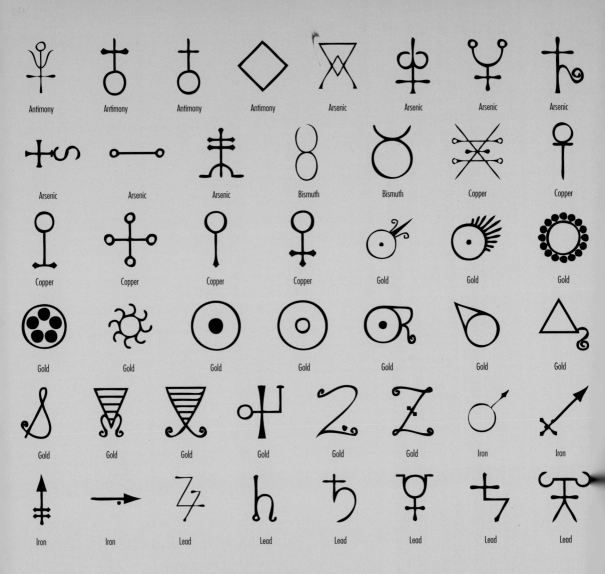

Antimony

Antimony

Antimony

Antimony

Arsenic

Arsenic

Arsenic

Arsenic

Arsenic

Arsenic

Arsenic

Bismuth

Bismuth

Copper

Copper

Copper

Copper

Copper

Copper

Gold

Gold

Gold

Gold

Gold

Gold

Gold

Gold

Gold

Gold

Gold

Gold

Gold

Gold

Gold

Gold

Iron

Iron

Iron

Iron

Lead

Lead

Lead

Lead

Lead

Lead

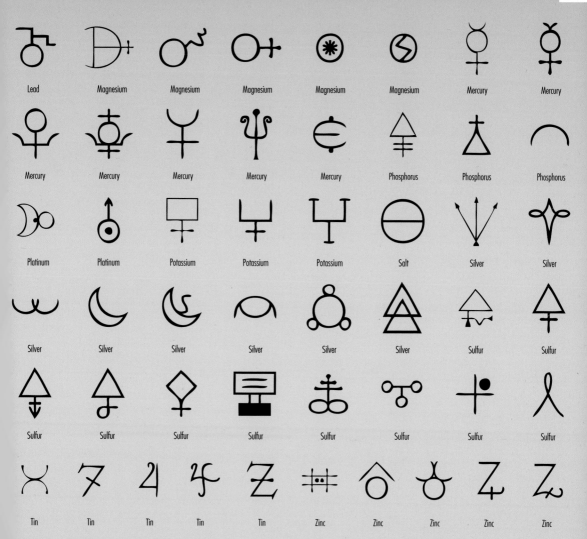

Lead	Magnesium	Magnesium	Magnesium	Magnesium	Magnesium	Mercury	Mercury
Mercury	Mercury	Mercury	Mercury	Mercury	Phosphorus	Phosphorus	Phosphorus
Platinum	Platinum	Potassium	Potassium	Potassium	Salt	Silver	Silver
Silver	Silver	Silver	Silver	Silver	Silver	Sulfur	Sulfur
Sulfur	Sulfur	Sulfur	Sulfur	Sulfur	Sulfur	Sulfur	Sulfur
Tin	Tin	Tin	Tin	Tin	Zinc	Zinc	Zinc	Zinc	Zinc

Membership and Identity

Membership and Identity

Instantly recognizable and memorable, signs and symbols are fundamental to indicating identity and membership. Coats of arms represent the archetypal identification system—using symbols to represent dynastic attributes and status. Less codified icons are adopted to represent towns, cities, countries, and cultures: famous inhabitants, iconic buildings, and indigenous species all feature.

Affiliation to a religion, a political party, or a gang is typically communicated through symbols—from the personal statement of a tattoo to the oppressive symbols of dictatorship. Simple pictograms or iconic portraits can represent human identity. Signatures are unique to every individual and the graffiti equivalent, the tag, offers an urban take on the identity theme.

040 Village sign for Salle in East Anglia.
041 Commemorative Formica tray from 1961 showing London icons.
042 Live Once tattoo from the "Logbook of Love" by Jenny Orel.
043 A symbol of Scotland—the thistle.
044 The Hidden Holocaust exhibition signage at the Műcsarnok exhibition space in Budapest.
045 Part of a set of Culture Cards by UMS Design Studio in Mumbai.
046 Virgin Atlantic brand book by Turner Duckworth.
047 Detail of a stars and stripes USA sign.
048 The luxurious China Club in Beijing combines traditional Chinese lanterns with the red star of communism to create a modern icon.
049 The bald eagle—the USA's national emblem since 1782.

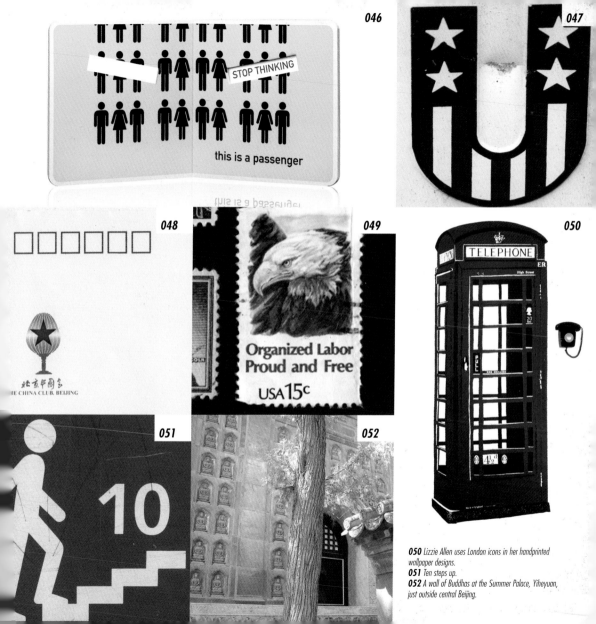

046

STOP THINKING

this is a passenger

047

048

北京中国会
THE CHINA CLUB, BEIJING

049

Organized Labor
Proud and Free

USA 15c

050

TELEPHONE

051

10

052

050 Lizzie Allen uses London icons in her handprinted
wallpaper designs.
051 Ten steps up.
052 A wall of Buddhas at the Summer Palace, Yiheyuan,
just outside central Beijing.

Coats of Arms

Developed during the Middle Ages, a coat of arms was a design on a knight's coat or on his shield—the only way of identifying him in full body armor. Countries, cities, families, regiments, even corporate entities and branded products employ coats of arms to reflect their identities, evoke heritage, and connote quality. Modern interpretations use varied iconography, but heraldry was originally governed by strict rules using Old French terms. Colors are argent (silver), or (gold), gules (red), and sable (black); the various patterns are referred to as "furs."

A full coat of arms has a shield, helmet, and crest, with supporters on either side (such as "lions rampant"), and a motto underneath. The shields can be divided into "fields," or by graphic devices such as a vertical cross, saltire (diagonal cross), pale (vertical line), or bend (diagonal line). The sections of the shield are decorated with devices called charges—figures of animals, plants, or objects. A popular motif is the fleur-de-lis—the stylized lily or iris design associated variously with the French monarchy, the Holy Trinity, and the Virgin Mary.

053 *Make your own coat of arms using these elements created by Andrey Pustovoy (crowns), David Luscombe (shield variations), Julie Felton (fleur-de-lis options), and a crest complete with winged horses by John Woodcock. (All sourced via istockphoto.com)*
Below the crest are shields which are divided into "fields." L/R: cross, saltire, pale, and bend.

Civic Signs

We tend to think of location branding as a modern phenomenon, but the English village sign is nearly a century old. In 1912 King Edward VII had signs erected in villages on the Sandringham estate in the county of Norfolk. The post-war years saw the practice really take hold, with ornately painted and carved signs cropping up at the entrances and on the greens of many of the country's picturesque villages. Don't be fooled by their aged look: many of these signs are new—with some put up to mark the millennium. Designed to reflect the history and heritage of the village, they depict local trades, legendary events, and famous inhabitants—Lord Nelson adorns the sign of his birthplace, Burnham Thorpe.

It may seem odd to compare English village signs with badges commemorating the towns and cities of Soviet-era Russia, but the purpose of these signs is essentially the same. From Burston's wholesome wheat sheaf to Zhelesnogorsk, site of the world's largest nuclear complex, these signs evoke civic pride, commemorate achievement, and idealize worlds.

054–059 A collection of village signs from around East Anglia photographed by Leo Reynolds.
060–068 Commemorative Russian enamel badges from the collection of Richard and Olga Davis. Top, L/R: Nevelisk, Dolinsk, Komsomolsk-on-Amur. Middle, L/R: Novosibirsk, Artyom, Kirov. Bottom, L/R: Berdychiv, Arsenyev, Zhelesnogorsk.

060 НЕВЕЛЬСК

061 ДОЛИНСК

062 КОМСОМОЛЬСК-НА-АМУРЕ

063 НОВОСИБИРСК

064 АРТЕМ

065 КИРОВ

066 БЕРДИЧЕВ

067 АРСЕНЬЕВ

068 ЖЕЛЕЗНОГОРСК ИЛИМСКИЙ

Tattoos

Evidence from petroglyphs and prehistoric burials indicates that tattooing, painting, and scarification were all practiced in ancient times to indicate membership of a tribe, to show allegiance to a god, for protection from evil or disease, and for pure aesthetics. The word "tattoo" originates from the Tahitian "tattau"—meaning "to mark." The Egyptians spread the practice of tattooing throughout the world and every culture has its take on the art. Notable are the Japanese, who perfected the use of color and perspective, and the Maori of New Zealand, who used their woodcarving skills to create the full-face "moko," a mark of distinction, indicating achievements in war and the great events of the wearer's life.

Mehndi is the ancient art of henna body painting. The tradition of creating elaborate designs on various parts of the body is considered good luck in India, the Middle East, and North Africa, and has formed an essential part of ceremonial preparation for 5,000 years. Patterns vary from culture to culture. In India, hands and feet are covered in intricate, lacy designs—typically seen on Indian brides—while more geometric patterns are favored in North Africa. →

069 An Indian bride's decorative henna hand tattoos photographed by Ashwin Kharidehal Abhirama.
070 Henna foot tattoos by Tom O'Connell.
071 Ta moko Maori tattoo photographed by Nicolette Neish.
072 Pauline Amphlett uses henna hand tattoo designs in this art piece.

070

071

072

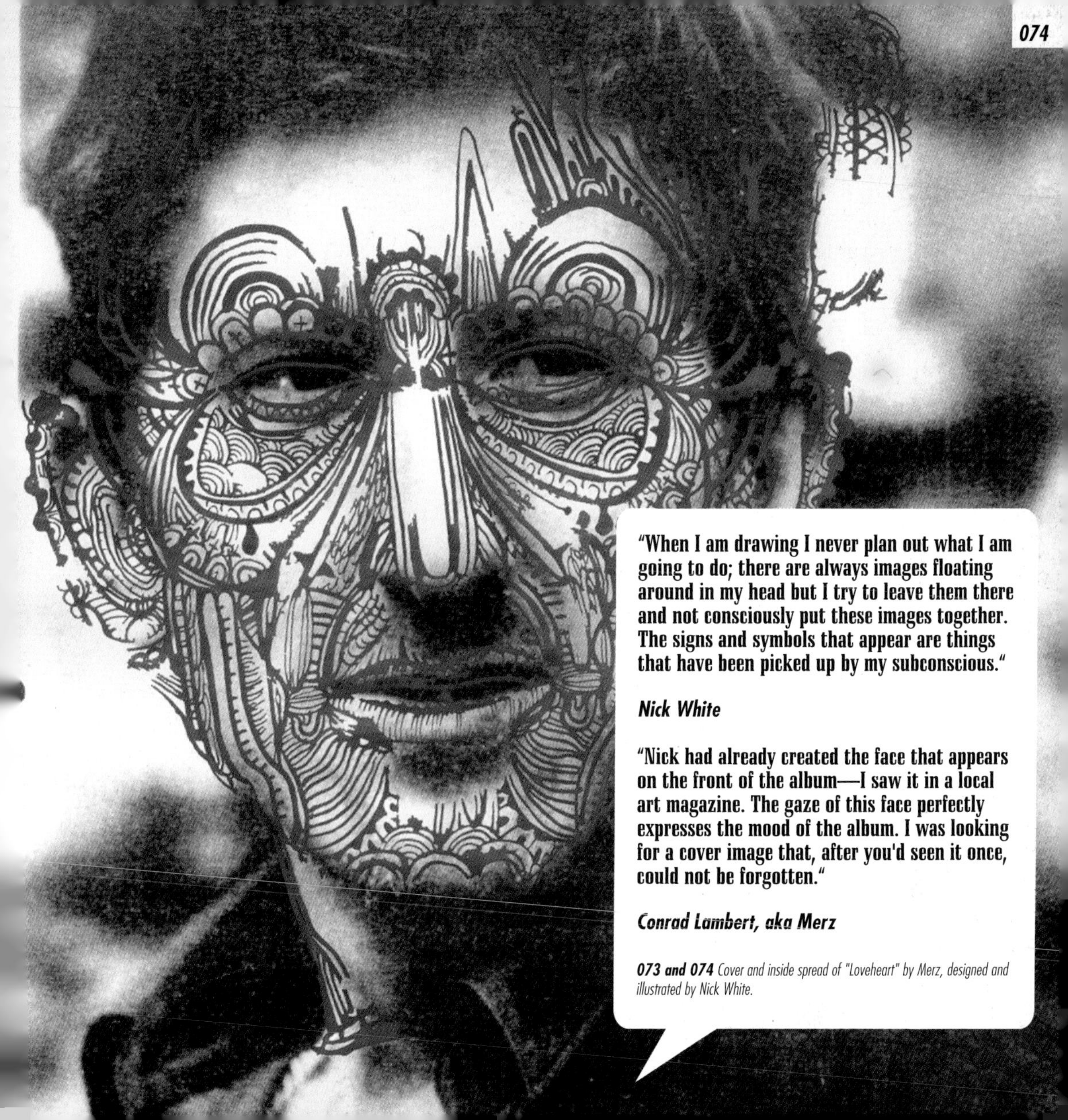

"When I am drawing I never plan out what I am going to do; there are always images floating around in my head but I try to leave them there and not consciously put these images together. The signs and symbols that appear are things that have been picked up by my subconscious."

Nick White

"Nick had already created the face that appears on the front of the album—I saw it in a local art magazine. The gaze of this face perfectly expresses the mood of the album. I was looking for a cover image that, after you'd seen it once, could not be forgotten."

Conrad Lambert, aka Merz

073 and 074 *Cover and inside spread of "Loveheart" by Merz, designed and illustrated by Nick White.*

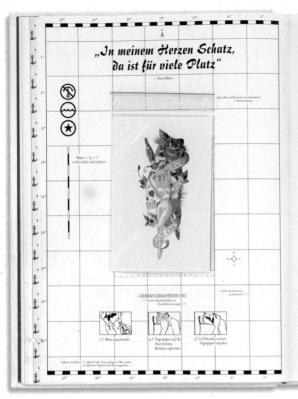

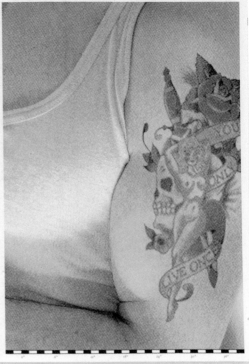

→ Sailors introduced tattoos to Europe, returning from exotic postings with their bodies adorned with flowers, hearts, and lovers' names; mermaids, ships, and anchors; snakes, dragons, and birds. Associations with the armed forces continue, though the reality is often less romantic: members of today's military sometimes have their identification tags tattooed onto their ribs—known as "meat tags."

The tattoo carries varied associations with identity and membership. In 19th-century Europe it was fashionable among some sections of the upper class to have discreet tattoos of family crests and other aristocratic emblems. At the other extreme, tattoos have also been long associated with criminals—either as state imposed identification symbols, or self-inscribed by inmates as an expression of autonomy. They can also indicate "dead time"—the number of years spent in prison. →

075 Spread from the "Logbook of Love" by Jenny Orel, featuring a pull out, rub down "sailor style" tattoo.
076 BMX biker with tattoo.
077 A traditional heart tattoo with scroll and Cupid's arrow.
078 Insert artwork for the "Loveheart" album by Merz, created by Nick White.
079 Captain Morgan Tattoo packaging with elaborate foiled tattoos designed by UK consultancy, Identica.
080 Scroll necklace by Comfort Station.
081–083 Inky icons of self-expression: tattoos reflect their wearers' individuality.

→ Gang membership is also expressed through tattoos—a permanent mark of allegiance to your pack. Motorcycle gangs immediately come to mind. Members of the Hell's Angels often have a tattoo of a patch with a skull wearing an aviator's cap set within a set of wings, while the Bandidos sometimes carry a 1% tattoo to indicate they are the one percent of true outlaws among the motorcycle fraternity.

For much of the 20th century they were the preserve of those "too lazy to work and too scared to steal," but the tattoo's associations with the fringes of society are being expropriated by the mainstream: over 60 percent of all North Americans aged 18 to 30 years old have at least one tattoo. Yet the tattoo remains a symbol of individuality— an expression of one's personality. Celebrities reveal their latest tattoos—the names of their children, wives, and lovers displayed in prominent places ripe for photo opportunities—while beneath respectable business suits, lawyers, accountants, and bankers harbor inky icons of self-expression in suitably discreet spots.

085

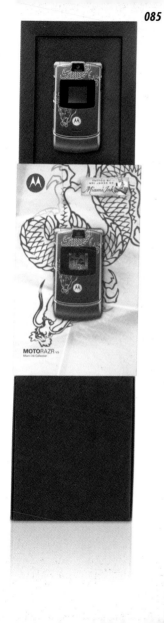

084 Sailors returning from the East introduced tattoos into Europe. A recurring tattoo motif is the swirling Chinese dragon which can wrap around the arm for a continuous pattern.
085 Turner Duckworth created this packaging for Motorola featuring the design work of tattoo artist Ami James of Tattoo Ink. Design: Shawn Rosenberger, Ann Jordan, Josh Michaels, Rebecca Williams, Brittany Hull, Radu Ranga. Product imagery: Paul Obleas, Motorola.
086 Sacred heart tattoo.
087 Butt Butt is a fun way to conserve rainwater—designed for Straight plc. by Gerardine and Wayne Hemingway, of Hemingway Design.
088 and 089 Tattoos at the base of the spine influenced the design icon feature on the Butt Butt water collector.

086

087

088

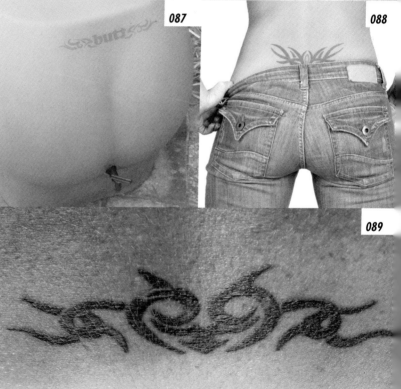

089

Tags

In 1979 art dealer Claudio Bruni gave New York graffiti artists Lee Quinones and Fab Five Freddy a gallery opening in Rome. It represented a reassessment of graffiti as an art form and the beginning of the gentrification of street art that has culminated in the worldwide cult of Banksy.

The "value" of the work might be shifting from the sidewalk to the art gallery, but a walk through London's Shoreditch or downtown Manhattan will testify that there's still plenty of activity on the streets. Tags have become intrinsic to the urban landscape. These elaborate identifiers—graffiti signatures, often inscrutable to the uninitiated—are part of the urban vernacular and are appropriated (whether in earnest or ironically) to lend an urban edge to design and communication.

090–095 Tags in the urban environment ranging from the basic to the elaborate.
096 The Gorillaz figures' packaging, by Kidrobot and The Gorillaz, has an urban flavor utilizing their spray paint tag-inspired logo.

097 This New York door has been tagged several times, creating a multicolored random pattern.
098 The classic tradition of Dutch Delft craftsmanship hits the streets of New York City with the New York Delft porcelain dinnerware collection by Lovegrove and Repucci.

099
100
101

City Icons

Built in 1889, during the belle epoque, the Eiffel Tower stood for all that was good about Paris at the time—a city leading the way in engineering, leisure, and culture. It also coincided with the rise of tourism, and was therefore pictured on a proliferation of souvenirs and postcards. So the Eiffel Tower set the precedent for the city icon. Easily depicted in two or three dimensions, it has come to represent the city of Paris.

Buildings, structures, and monuments create an instant association with the look and feel of a city, its culture and values, and are therefore ripe for graphic appropriation. They might be contemporary structures, like the London Eye, erected with the goal of achieving iconic status, or everyday objects that come to signify their unique location, like New York's rooftop water towers. →

099 The iconic Empire State Building represented in its own entrance hall.
100 The unmistakable arches of the Brooklyn Bridge.
101 The Brooklyn Bridge featured on this T-shirt design by Brooklyn Industries.
102–104 The elaborate onion-shaped domes of St. Basil's Cathedral in Moscow have become symbols of the city.
105–107 The unmistakable water towers of New York—without which there would not be enough pressure to allow water utilities to function—add to the skyline and to the design palette of Brooklyn Industries, who incorporated the towers into their illustrated cityscape identity.

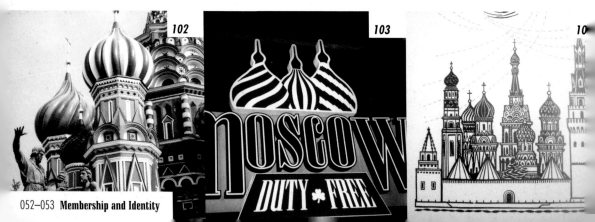

102
103
10

BROOKLYN INDUSTRIES

→ While tourism bolstered the phenomenon of the city icon, many of the buildings and sights that represent cities predate and supersede tourism. The onion domes of Moscow's St. Basil's, the gondolas of Venice, and the rising bascules of London's Tower Bridge are each intrinsic to their respective cities and make fitting icons, but they weren't created with this as their primary goal.

Increasingly, however, metropolitan authorities, keen to promote their cities, commission buildings with the intention of raising their profile on the world stage. Height plays a key strategic role. The gauntlet thrown down by the Empire State building in 1931 (for over 40 years the world's tallest building) has been picked up by architects, town planners, and city officials ever since, with ever taller buildings designed to achieve iconic status for their host cities.

108 *Venetian gondolier.*
109 *Seattle's Space Needle was created for the 1962 World's Fair, offering visitors a glimpse of the future.*
110 *Created in its likeness: traditional woodturner, artist, and Washington resident Richard Steppic individually hand crafts "Space Needle" pepper mills.*
111–113 *Icons of Cadiz by design company Salvartes Estudio de Diseño y Publicidad. Featured L/R: Puertas De Tierra, Castillo De San Sebastian, Torreon.*
114 *London's Tower Bridge.*
115 *Simplified image of Westminster and the clock tower housing Big Ben.*
016 *A commemorative £2 coin, featuring searchlights and the dome of London's St Paul's Cathedral.*
017 *Designer Lizzie Allen celebrates St Paul's Cathedral in this wallpaper design.*

114

115

116

117

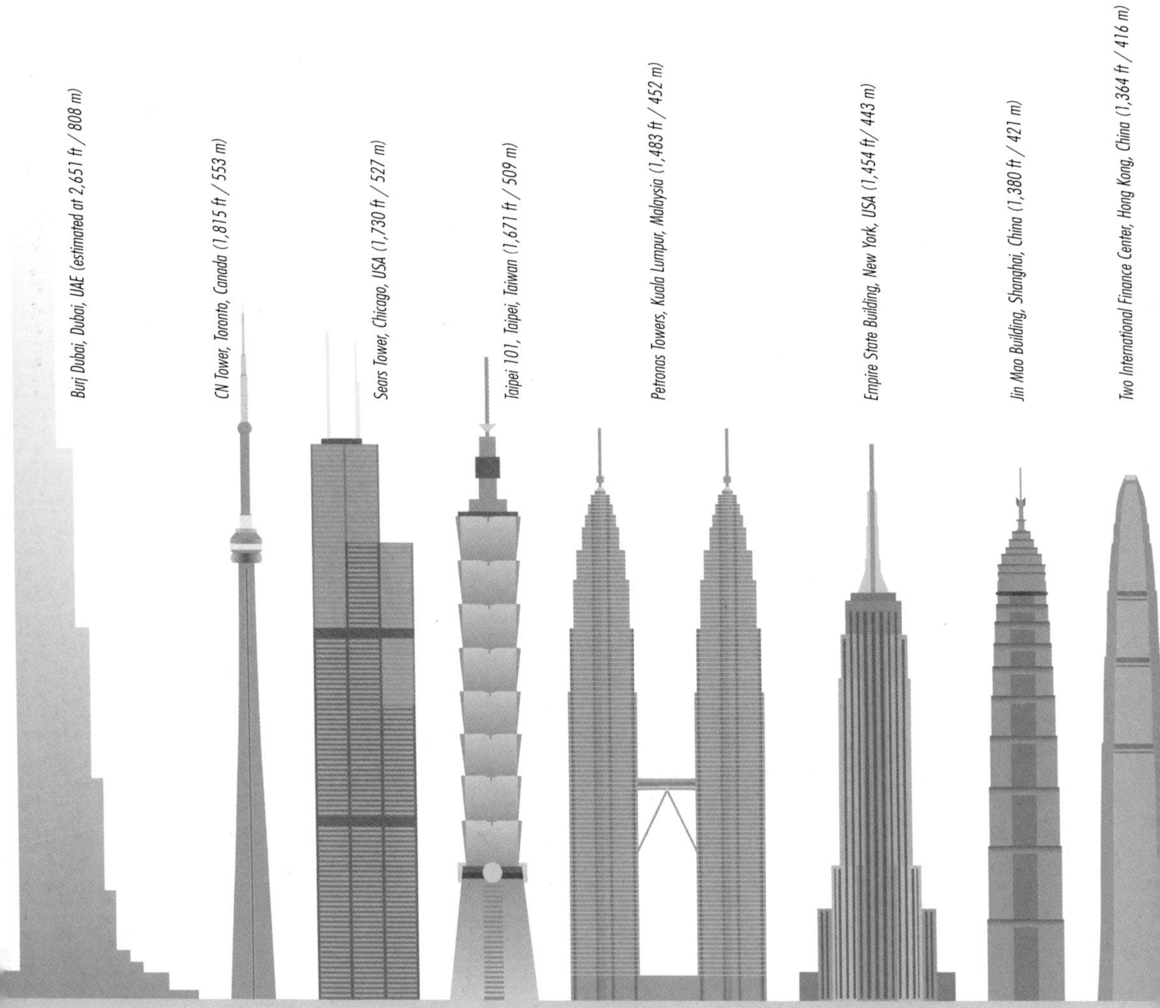

Burj Dubai, Dubai, UAE (estimated at 2,651 ft / 808 m)

CN Tower, Toronto, Canada (1,815 ft / 553 m)

Sears Tower, Chicago, USA (1,730 ft / 527 m)

Taipei 101, Taipei, Taiwan (1,671 ft / 509 m)

Petronas Towers, Kuala Lumpur, Malaysia (1,483 ft / 452 m)

Empire State Building, New York, USA (1,454 ft / 443 m)

Jin Mao Building, Shanghai, China (1,380 ft / 421 m)

Two International Finance Center, Hong Kong, China (1,364 ft / 416 m)

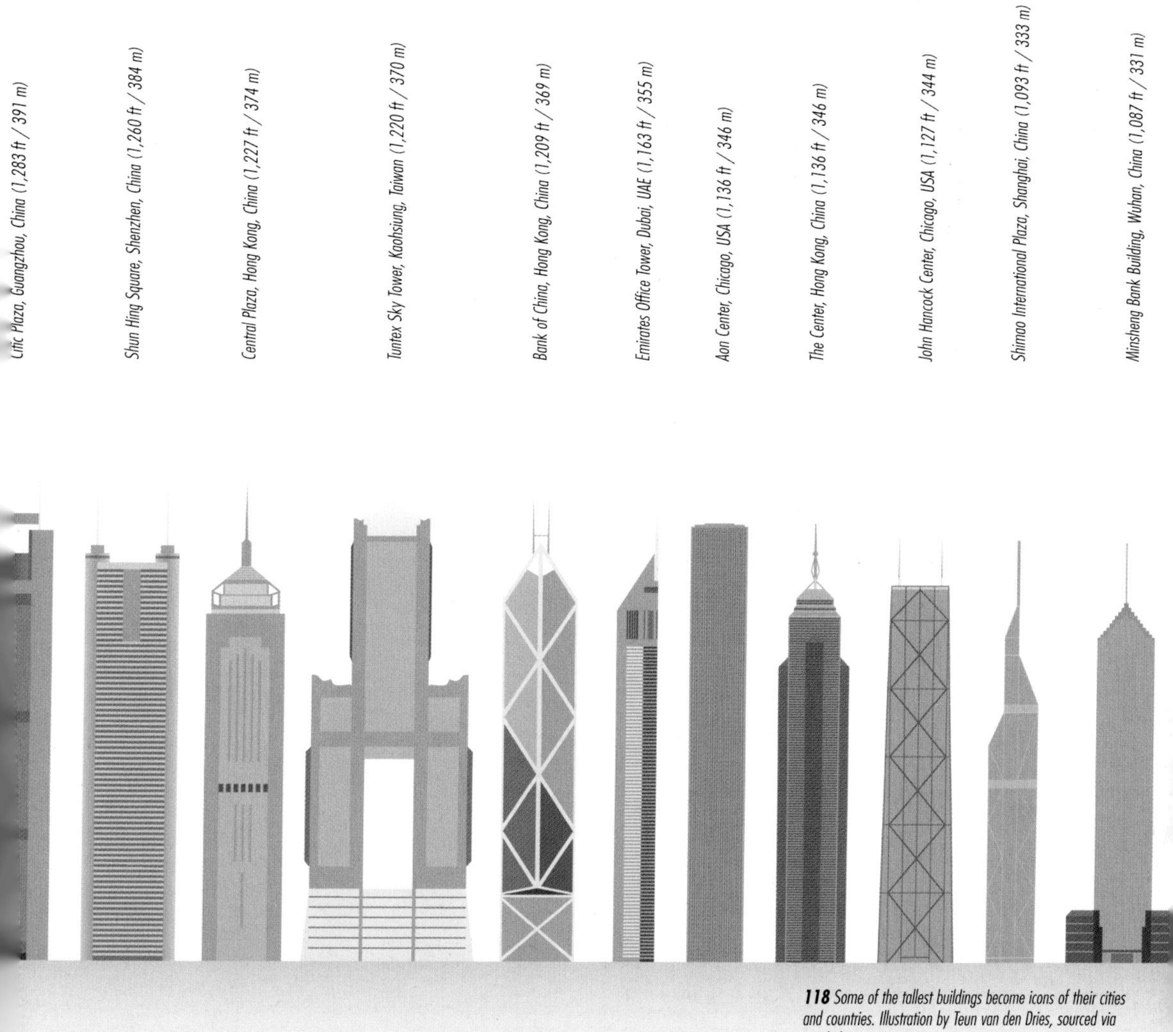

CITIC Plaza, Guangzhou, China (1,283 ft / 391 m)

Shun Hing Square, Shenzhen, China (1,260 ft / 384 m)

Central Plaza, Hong Kong, China (1,227 ft / 374 m)

Tuntex Sky Tower, Kaohsiung, Taiwan (1,220 ft / 370 m)

Bank of China, Hong Kong, China (1,209 ft / 369 m)

Emirates Office Tower, Dubai, UAE (1,163 ft / 355 m)

Aon Center, Chicago, USA (1,136 ft / 346 m)

The Center, Hong Kong, China (1,136 ft / 346 m)

John Hancock Center, Chicago, USA (1,127 ft / 344 m)

Shimao International Plaza, Shanghai, China (1,093 ft / 333 m)

Minsheng Bank Building, Wuhan, China (1,087 ft / 331 m)

118 Some of the tallest buildings become icons of their cities and countries. Illustration by Teun van den Dries, sourced via istockphoto.com.

Countries and Cultures

The symbols that represent countries on flags, coats of arms, and airplane tailfins are largely derived from geography and natural history. Flora and fauna commonly feature. As a nation of gardeners, it's hardly surprising that Britain represents its countries as plants. Canada brands everything from its airline to its ice hockey team with the ubiquitous maple leaf. Australia and New Zealand look to their indigenous kangaroo and kiwi to create distinctiveness.

After the collapse of the Soviet Union, the Russian government considered adopting a bear as the new national symbol—but the Tsarist double-headed eagle won in the end. The bald eagle was officially declared the national emblem of the United States as far back as 1782. A species unique to North America, it has since become symbolic of the USA's self-image as a land of freedom. Hence, the country symbol has been imbued with cultural values.　　　　→

119 Patron saint of England and a dozen or more countries besides, St. George is depicted killing the dragon.
120 Coin to commemorate the tercentenary of the Act of Union between England and Scotland, featuring the English rose and the Scottish thistle.
121 A stylized English rose.
122 The lion is a frequently used British symbol.
123 The gates of London's Marble Arch feature the lion.
124 The Welsh dragon.
125–128 The English rose, the Scottish thistle, the Irish shamrock, and the Welsh leek: wall paintings in the cloisters of Norwich Cathedral, UK, seen by Leo Reynolds.

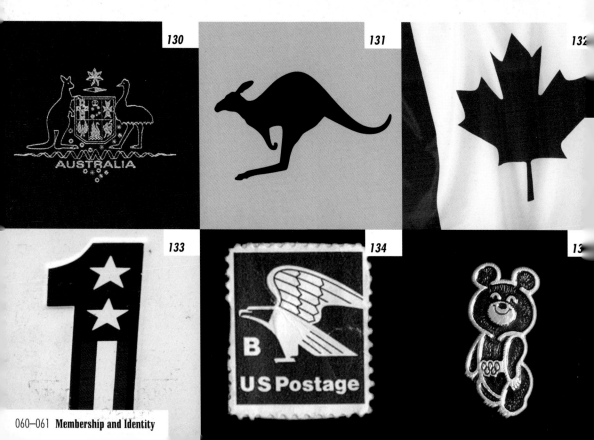

130

AUSTRALIA

131

132

133

134

13

129 Souvenirs of Canada—maple leaf spinning tops in maple wood, by Patty Johnson. Created for the Cabin Project, whose aim was to celebrate Canada and its best new design talent.
130 and 131 Symbols of Australia—the kangaroo and the emu.
132 Canadian maple leaf.
133 and 134 Symbols of the USA—the stars and stripes and the bald eagle.
135 This Russian bear character, Misha, was the mascot for the 1980 Moscow Olympics.
136 The icon for Russian Standard vodka, created by Identica, mixes the Russian bear and Tsarist eagle to offer unmistakably Russian cues.
137 A traditional Chinese dragon outside the Forbidden City in Beijing.
138 The New Zealand kiwi.

→ Many countries take steps to manage their national brands—how the rest of the world perceives them. France is all about fashion, Denmark is known for design, Germany for automotive engineering. A country's culture is in a perpetual state of flux, influenced by economic and political circumstances, immigration, and societal trends; so the symbols that sum up cultural identity are always shifting and changing. Cultural identity holds reality and cliché in fine balance; artists and designers can take cultural icons and subvert them to create work that comments on a country's self-image and the nature of stereotypes.

"Our illustration highlights the recent trend analysis conducted by Trend Group, on how Latin American and Turkish cultures are close to each other. For the main identity and illustration, we combined one of Latin America's famous icons with a mustache, which represents the Turkish stereotype."

Can Burak Bizer,
2Fresh

136 Istanbul-based design agency 2Fresh's illustration for Trend Group.
137 UMS Design Studio, based in Mumbai, created this Culture Cards game for the International Centre of Ethnographic Studies. The part-image cards create a full image set when questions about the culture, practices, and customs of the people of India are correctly answered.

"LATİN AMERİKA NE KADAR UZAK?"

141

142

143

144

1

064–065 **Membership and Identity**

OLD TOWN

Including
Tin House Workwear Favourites

www.old-town.co.uk

£102.00
£102.00
£150.00

4–145 *Lowri Davies uses her Welsh heritage as a major* *rce of inspiration. Her ceramics embrace Welsh cultural* *eotypes using iconic figures in traditional Welsh dress, seen* *ieces like Chat and Hiraethu am yr henebion (Longing for* *Old and the Traditional). The work stems from references* *hina displays on Welsh dressers and ceramic souvenirs.*

6 and 147 *Old Town create a nostalgic vision of Britain* *celebrate bygone days with their high quality fabrics and* *ing design. Above is one of their Tin House workwear* *rites, the bungalow dress in Pavillion fabric, which* *res icons of the British seaside: tea pots, sunshades,* *ncomfortable, wrought iron guest-house beds. Their* *ure and gift wrap design continue the theme, using* *of Britishness, including umbrellas, more tea, a vintage* *hone, and the old General Post Office crown icon,* *gest its mail order use.*

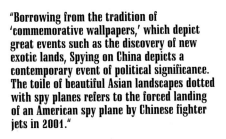

"Borrowing from the tradition of 'commemorative wallpapers,' which depict great events such as the discovery of new exotic lands, Spying on China depicts a contemporary event of political significance. The toile of beautiful Asian landscapes dotted with spy planes refers to the forced landing of an American spy plane by Chinese fighter jets in 2001."

Jennifer Smith, artist,
in collaboration with Studio Printworks

148 *Spying on China wallpaper.*
149–151 *Taking the traditional Willow Pattern plate decoration, artist Robert Dawson reworks the familiar design into abstract icon pieces by enlarging the design and distorting the perspectives. These are three of the eight plates in a collection entitled: Can you walk from the Garden, does your heart understand.*
152 *In Persepctive Willow 1.*

149

150

151

152

153 · **154** · **155**

DAS BESTE DESIGN
DES JAHRHUNDERTS

Political Symbols

Today's political parties use symbols to communicate their values and engender loyalty. There are doves and red roses, sunflowers and elephants, even donkeys. An example of the perceived influence of these symbols is the UK Conservative Party's recent switch from a patriotic torch (too aggressive) to an oak tree (solid and eco-friendly).

But it's all pretty innocuous stuff in comparison to the major political powers of the 20th century, which adopted potent symbolic branding. Hitler's hijacking of the swastika proved to be the most dreadful of misappropriations, turning a life-asserting symbol of the Hindu, Jain, and Buddhist religions into the most reviled symbol in western culture. Even decades after the demise of the Nazis, it remains a crime to display the swastika in Germany. →

153–157 Hitler's Nazi Party adopted the swastika (in German: Hakenkreuz) at the height of its widespread popular use. They rotated it 45 degrees and used it in the red, white, and black colors of the old German Empire flag to create strong nationalistic associations.
158 An anti-nazi symbol showing the swastika being thrown in the trash—inspired by the Keep Britain Tidy icon.

156 · **1**

→ Hitler's party understood the power of graphic symbolism. Concentration camp prisoners were branded with symbols to identify the reason for their internment. Most infamous is the yellow Star of David used to identify Jewish prisoners, but this was just one in a system of symbols using colored fabric triangles—chosen for their warning quality—sewn on to uniforms in a variety of formations, each carrying a chilling significance. The addition of a sewn target meant the wearer was an escape suspect.

Despite the steady demise of communism around the world, its symbols live on in our cultural consciousness. While Mongolia revels in replacing the oppressive hammer and sickle with icons of their spiritual leader, Chinggis Khan, modern Russians regard the hammer and sickle with ambivalence. Despite fervent modernization, the symbol was retained by national airline Aeroflot as a badge of honor for its pilots. Meanwhile, China's red star is incorporated into the work of contemporary Chinese artists and designers who now enjoy the freedom to subvert its authoritarian associations.

159 A chart of prisoner markings used in German concentration camps. Sourced from the United States Holocaust Memorial Museum.
160 The Hidden Holocaust exhibition signage at the Műcsarnok exhibition space in Budapest shows badges that were given to concentration camp prisoners during WWII. Housed in a black triangle (standing for asocial elements such as vagrants and the mentally ill), are a brown triangle (used for Roma and Sinti), a pink triangle (gay males), a purple triangle (immigrants), a yellow star (Jews), and a red triangle (political enemies).

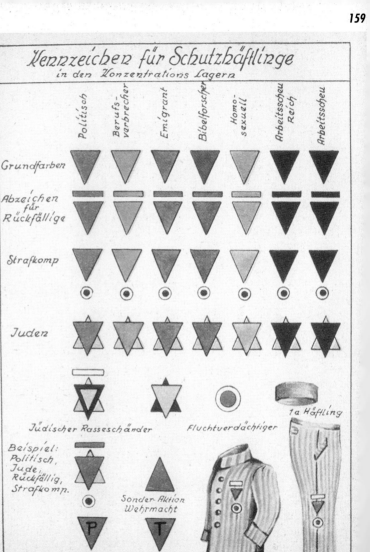

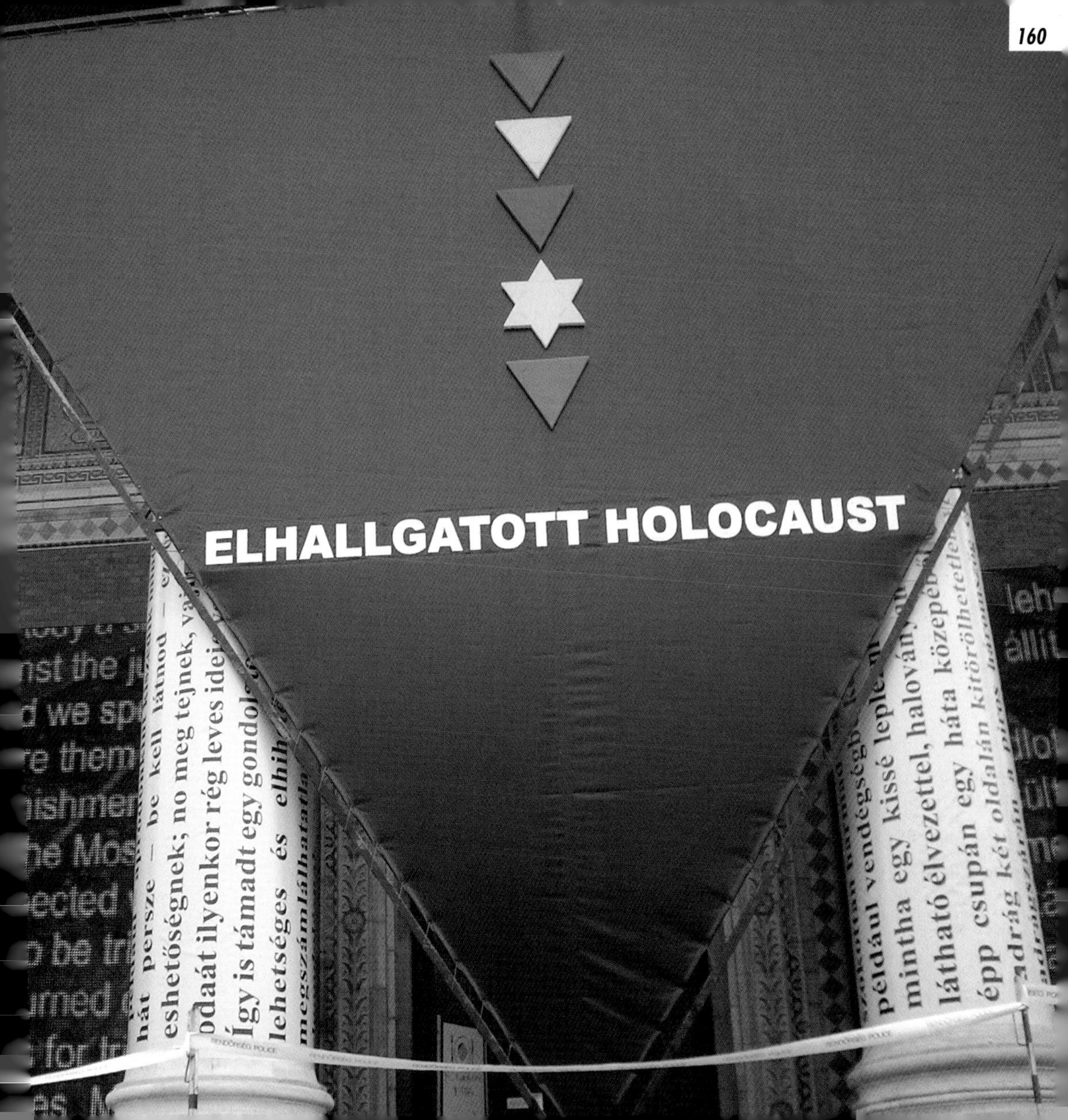
ELHALLGATOTT HOLOCAUST

161 People's statue on Tiananmen Square.

162 and 167 The contemporary art scene in China is thriving and in the Dashanzi art district the old communist symbols of stars and even of Mao himself are being used as cool icons.

163 This Chinese fashion label uses the traditional iconography of communist China with retro irony to brand its clothes.

164 and 165 A market in Beijing sells communist paraphernalia to tourists, including copies of Mao's "Little Red Book" and figurines marking the Cultural Revolution.

166 The stylish uniforms worn by the staff of The Commune by the Great Wall hotel are reminiscent of the traditional Zhongshan Zhuang, or Mao suit.

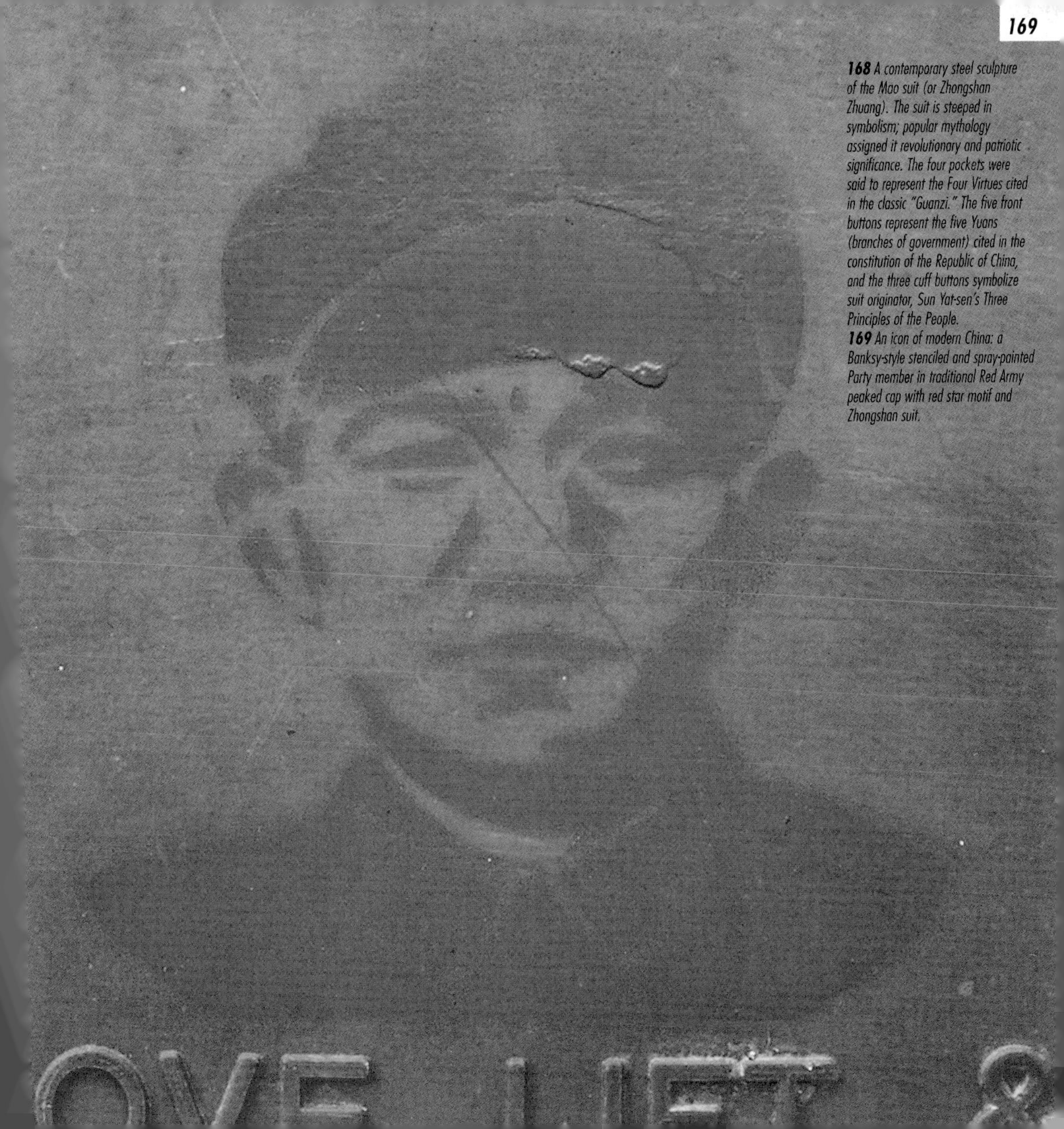

168 A contemporary steel sculpture of the Mao suit (or Zhongshan Zhuang). The suit is steeped in symbolism; popular mythology assigned it revolutionary and patriotic significance. The four pockets were said to represent the Four Virtues cited in the classic "Guanzi." The five front buttons represent the five Yuans (branches of government) cited in the constitution of the Republic of China, and the three cuff buttons symbolize suit originator, Sun Yat-sen's Three Principles of the People.

169 An icon of modern China: a Banksy-style stenciled and spray-painted Party member in traditional Red Army peaked cap with red star motif and Zhongshan suit.

171

173

175

172

174

176

177

170 The coat of arms of the former Lithuanian Soviet Socialist Republic features the hammer and sickle.

171 A meeting of Soyombo—the traditional symbol of Mongolia—and the hammer and sickle of Soviet Russia.

172 A statue of Lenin remains as a symbol of Mongolia's Soviet past.

173–176 Soviet badges from the collection of Richard and Ira Davis, featuring powerful communist symbols such as the star, the red flag, the hammer and sickle, and the head of Lenin.

177 Soviet propagandist art, situated just outside Ulanbaatar, Mongolia.

Religious Symbols

It may sound like heresy, but commercial branding can learn a few lessons from religious symbology. The clarity and simplicity of religious iconography does everything that modern brands aspire to do: creating a trusted mark with the power to unite people in a set of shared beliefs and values. Put simply, these are logos—graphic representations designed for easy recognition. Religious symbols may be drawn from the accoutrements of religious ritual, such as the stylized arch of the torii gate at the entrance to Shinto shrines, or involve a deeper level of interpretation, as in the Jain hand, which represents the doctrine of Ahimsa.

Religions employ a range of icons and symbols to represent their tenets. As one of the best-known Hindu deities, Ganesha acts as a symbol of the faith; images of Ganesha are rich in symbolism, representing ideas and qualities key to Hinduism, and created according to a strict set of codified rules. The symbols of religion can take on broader cultural significance too: as well as representing the Jewish faith, the Star of David has become a symbol of Israel, and is associated with the Zionist movement.

178 Religious symbols. Top, L/R: Christian cross, Jewish Star of David, Hindu Aumkar. Middle, L/R: Islamic star and crescent, Buddhist Wheel of Dharma, Shinto Torii. Bottom, L/R: Sikh Khanda, Bahá'í star, Jain Ahimsa Symbol.
179 One of the earliest Christian symbols was that of a fish. In Greek, the phrase, "Jesus Christ, Son of God Savior," is "Iesous Christos Theou Yios Soter." The first letters of each of these Greek words, when put together, spell "ichthys," the Greek word for "fish" (ICQUS).
180 Symbol of the Church of England.
181 Stained glass from the Octagon Unitarian Chapel, Norwich, UK, featuring the Unitarian flaming chalice surrounded by symbols of six faiths. Made by Stephen Pask, 1999.

THIS CHURCH IS OPEN

182 New Buddha statue in Ulaanbaatar.
183 Virgin Mary candles at Notre Dame, Paris.
184 Christ statue with halo and sacred heart.
185 The Islamic symbol of the crescent moon on the dome
of Central Birmingham Mosque, UK.
186 Hindu Ganesha icons.
187 The Jewish Star of David appears on this Menorah.
188 This issue of design magazine "I.D.," includes articles
on new religious architecture and design, and features an i-Pod
shuffle in the form of a crucifix on its cover.
189 A Hindu shrine at the Batu Caves in Kuala Lumpur.
190 The symbolism of Ganesha.

the International Design Magazine *God=Details* .... **Houston Megachurch** .... **Laser Buddhas**
hovah's Contractors .... **Modernist Mosque** .... **Shabbat Technology** .... **Ideal Meditation Rooms**

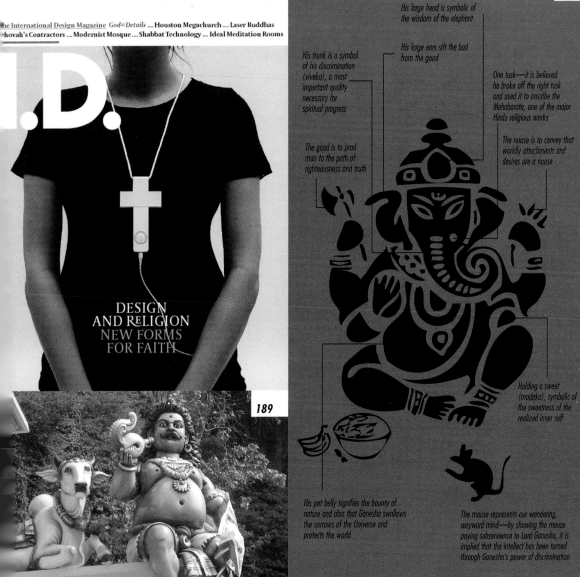

I.D.

DESIGN
AND RELIGION
NEW FORMS
FOR FAITH

His large head is symbolic of
the wisdom of the elephant

His large ears sift the bad
from the good

His trunk is a symbol
of his discrimination
(viveka), a most
important quality
necessary for
spiritual progress

One tusk—it is believed
he broke off the right tusk
and used it to inscribe the
Mahabarata, one of the major
Hindu religious works

The goad is to prod
man to the path of
righteousness and truth

The noose is to convey that
worldly attachments and
desires are a noose

Holding a sweet
(modaka), symbolic of
the sweetness of the
realized inner self

His pot belly signifies the bounty of
nature and also that Ganesha swallows
the sorrows of the Universe and
protects the world

The mouse represents our wandering,
wayward mind—by showing the mouse
paying subservience to Lord Ganesha, it is
implied that the intellect has been tamed
through Ganesha's power of discrimination

Human Identity

Way beyond the asteroid belt, over 8 billion miles away, Pioneer 10 has been famed throughout its 30-year mission as the most remote object ever made by man. Contact has now been lost with Pioneer 10 but it carries with it a significant testimonial of human existence: a pictorial plaque, designed to show scientifically educated inhabitants of another star system, who might intercept it millions of years from now, when Pioneer was launched, from where, and by what kind of beings.

Pioneer 10's plaque depicts a man and woman in front of an outline of the spacecraft. The man's hand is raised in a gesture of good will. The physical makeup of the man and woman were determined from results of a computerized analysis of the average person in our civilization—so they might be considered Mr. and Mrs. Average. They highlight the issues of symbolically representing human identity: the conundrum of reducing 6.6 billion individual identities to a homogeneous mean. →

191 and 192 *Walk and Don't Walk figures.*
193 *The human figure in the Universe. The Pioneer 10 design is etched into a 6 by 9 inch (15.2 by 22.8 cm) gold-anodized aluminum plate with representative male and female figures. Across the bottom are the planets, ranging outward from the Sun, with the spacecraft trajectory arching away from Earth, passing Mars, and swinging by Jupiter. The plaque was designed by Dr. Carl Sagan and Dr. Frank Drake and drawn by Linda Salzman Sagan.*

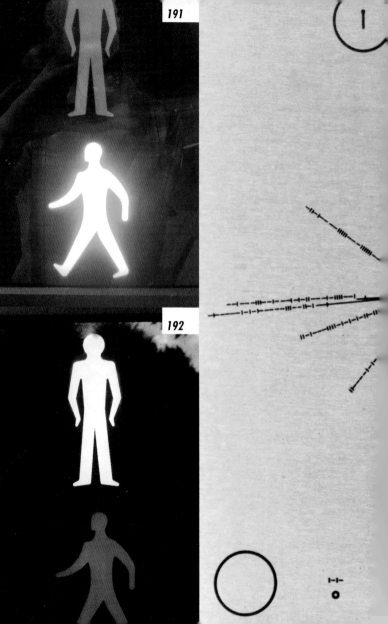

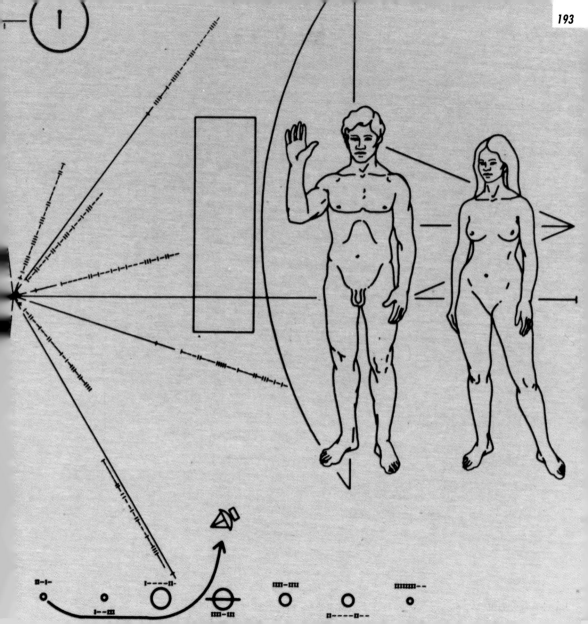

→ Most pictograms do away with any defining features for obvious reasons. Matters of individuality would hinder the directness of communication for which these icons are designed. Figurative representation is reduced to head, body, arms, and legs; sometimes just a head and body suffice. In many public environments, signage is required to indicate facilities for separate sexes. In these cases, the man and woman have to be differentiated—the woman might wear a dress, sometimes conjoining her legs represents her feminine stance. All solutions are fraught with risk. Differentiating through clothing opens up issues of both fashion (they'll date too quickly) and stereotyping (why should a woman wear a dress?). →

194 *Virgin Airlines brand book designed by Turner Duckworth.*
195 *Occasionally, cultural aspects are incorporated into pictograms, such as these male and female signs designed for Indian public hospitals by Ravi Poovaiah.*
196 and 198–200 *Figurative signage enables the viewer to immediately respond to whatever information or direction is being indicated—including differentiation between male and female washrooms, direction of stairs or escalator, and location of disability facilities.*
197 *Cut and Go Adam and Eve towel hanger designed by Julian Appelius for Pulpo.*

195

→ Using human figures in a wayfinding system suggests interaction, helping to personalize the built environment. While pictograms seek to create homogeneity, abstract figurative representations can suggest infinite variety of shape and form. Figurative icons can be the opposite of average. They can humanize, indicate movement and vibrancy, and celebrate difference.

Which brings us back to those 6.6 billion individuals. Of course, the only way to truly represent individual human identity is through faces. Even facial features can be drawn in a symbolic manner to create a graphic feel. Famous people are commonly referred to as "icons" and their features are often pared down to a limited number of elements to ensure instant recognition, emphasizing their iconic status.

201 Directional signage in this modern office and retail area in Beijing puts the human figure at the heart of the complex.

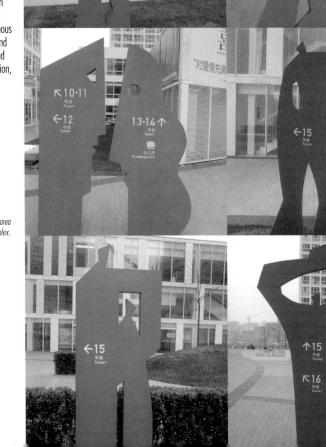

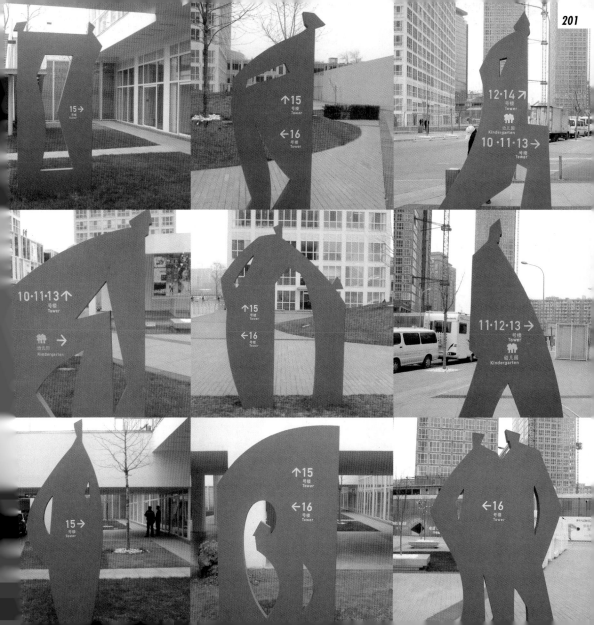

202–209 Some faces, for good or bad, achieve iconic sta
Featured here: Michael Jackson, Elvis, George Bush, Martin
Luther King, Bill Cosby, Alex from "A Clockwork Orange," Jir
Hendrix, and Uma Thurman in cult movie, "Pulp Fiction."
210 Detail of Nick White's poster containing 443 different
heads, which combines found imagery with his distinctive
illustrative style.

Themes and Moods

Themes and Moods

Signs and symbols offer a ready-made palette for communicating a vast array of themes and moods. For the designer and public alike, they act as visual shorthand for a universally understood language: a heart means love, a dove means peace, a chimney means industry, a rocket means space. This expedites messaging and allows creativity to be channeled toward the more nuanced aspects of communication.

The beauty of signs and symbols is that they can be generic found images: there are off-the-shelf icons and pictogram typefaces of everything from airplanes to Christmas trees, laundry symbols to sports icons. All of them can be used straight to communicate a theme per se, or customized, subverted, and remixed in a signs and symbols mash-up reflecting the diverse themes of modern life.

211 I Love New York.
212 Rainbow-colored CND symbol.
213 The Jolly Roger.
214 The exterior of this hardware store visually represesnts the tools and components available inside.
215 A lucky horseshoe.
216 Lance Wyman's icon for stamps and posters celebrating Mexico's 1970 FIFA World Cup.
217 This poster by Decoder for the band, Built to Spill, features love hearts exploding from a volcano. Designed by Christian Helms.
218 Factory icon used to promote Beijing's 798 district's art bienalle. The symbol reflects the area's industrial past before it became the innovative creative hub of the city.
219 Enid Seeny's 1950s Homemaker plate design for Woolworths.
220 A stylized bird by artist Wendy Earle.

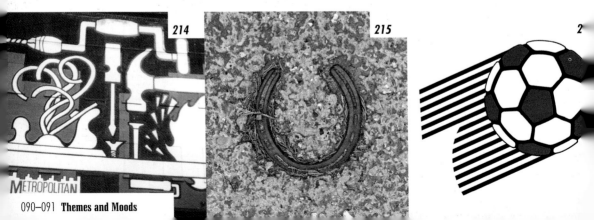

SATURDAY, SEPTEMBER 24TH AT LAZONA ROSA * WITH THOSE INCENDIARY INFIDELS THE DECEMBERISTS AND SONS AND DAUGHTERS

POSTER WITH LOVE BY CHRISTIAN@THEDECODERRING.COM

BIENNALE 79X

Hearts

When graphic designer Milton Glaser created the now legendary "I Love New York" logo in 1977 he intended it to support an advertising campaign for a few months. Four decades on, the logo is still going strong and stands as a benchmark for successful location branding. Following the 9/11 terrorist attacks, Glaser revised the logo in a defiant act of unity with the city and its people, adding the words "more than ever" and a dot in the heart to represent the location of the World Trade Center in Manhattan.

The logo is a good example of a rebus: where signs and symbols are used to replace a word or the syllables of a word. Featured on Valentines cards, public signs, even a brand of confectionary (with each sweet featuring a heart and a message such as "Be Mine"), the heart symbol is rarely interpreted as the word "heart," almost always as the word "love." Hearts are also commonly used more literally to symbolize health and wellbeing, but love is the most prevalent theme associated with them. "Wearing your heart on your sleeve" suggests expressing emotions freely and openly and, thematically, the heart is usually adopted to stand for romantic rather than passionate love.

221 A souvenir of an exciting city. The Milton Glaser design has become a global icon.
222–224 This collection of T-shirts by UK-based Product of Your Environment subverts the classic "I Love NY" icon with additions such as "I Love NYone," "I Love MoNeY," and "I Love my poNY."

Baked with Love.

225–227 Leo Reynolds' collection of hearts in the environment ranging from publicity for a bar to a restaurant promotion.
228 Wearing your heart on your sweater. Declaring a passion for the Beatles.

229 Tracy Dobbins' I Love Fat Chicks tote bag.
230 Declare your love for your favorite holiday season with these Christmas tree decorations.
231 Baked with Love bakery identity by Meat and Potatoes.

232 A blank Loveheart candy.
233 Wear your heart on your sleeve. Decoder's Christain Helms promotional poster for a concert by The Shins, inspired by the personal, confessional nature of the band's lyrics.
234 A graffiti heart.
235 Captured by Leo Reynolds, this icon dots the "i" with love

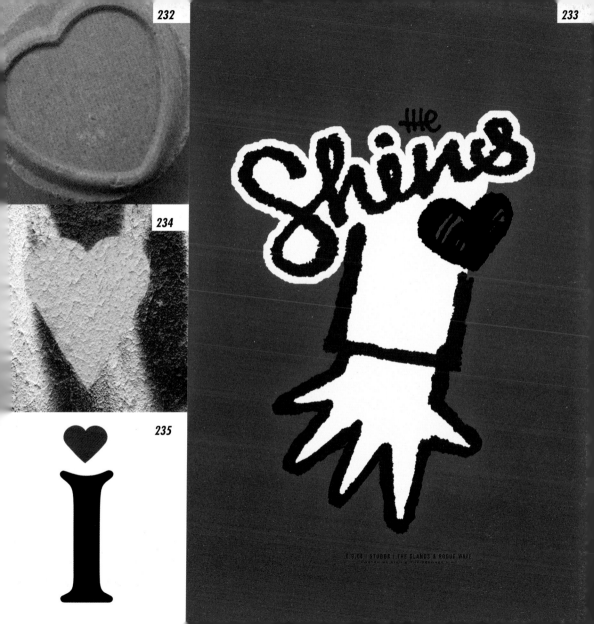

232

233

234

235

the Shins

8.9.03 | STUBBS / THE GLANDS & ROGUE WAVE

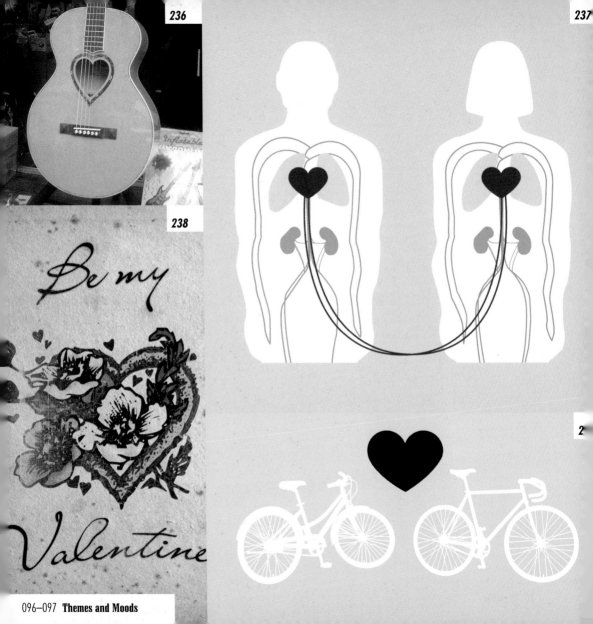

Be my

Valentine

236 A guitar that only plays romantic music?

237 Anatomical limited-edition poster for Hybrid Design by artist Dora Drimalas.

238 A vintage Valentine's message.

239 Bike Love limited-edition poster for Hybrid Design by artist Dora Drimalas.

240–241 Jewelry and accessories designers, Comfort Station, use cut-out hearts in their collection of necklaces and earrings.

242 The Hold Steady tour poster designed by Christian Helms for Recoder to support the release of "Boys and Girls in America." The album explores themes of youth, love, and drug culture. At its center is a line from Jack Kerouac, on which the poster is based.

240

241

242

War and Peace

Founded by Yuji Tokuda and Junya Ishikawa, an art director and a producer, both from Japan, Retired Weapons is a global collaboration that aims to spread the message of peace through the medium of design. They describe the campaign, which has brought together members of the creative community from across the world, as "a gentle yet powerful and very positive message." Visually, the campaign combines symbols of weapons with flowers— the notion of "retiring" weapons acknowledging the reality of war, while encouraging peaceful resistance. The campaign reflects the actions of the original "flower children" of the 1960s: anti-Vietnam campaigners who used the symbolism of flowers to promote their ideology of non-violence, giving flowers to policemen and putting flowers into the rifle barrels of members of the Reserve Officers' Training Corps.

War and peace signs and symbols fall into a poignant juxtaposition of man-made versus natural. Rifles, grenades, tanks, and planes all represent war, while hearts, flowers, and doves stand for peace. The poppy was chosen as a symbol of remembrance because of the poppies that bloomed on the Flanders battlefields in WWI, their red color an appropriate symbol for the bloodshed of trench warfare. The now internationally recognized peace symbol was originally created by British artist and pacifist, Gerald Holtom, to accompany the 1958 anti-nuclear march from London to Aldermaston.

243–246 *Images of the London installation of Retired Weapons featuring their iconic weaponry with flowers and the centerpiece tank with inflatable flowers.*

retired weapons™

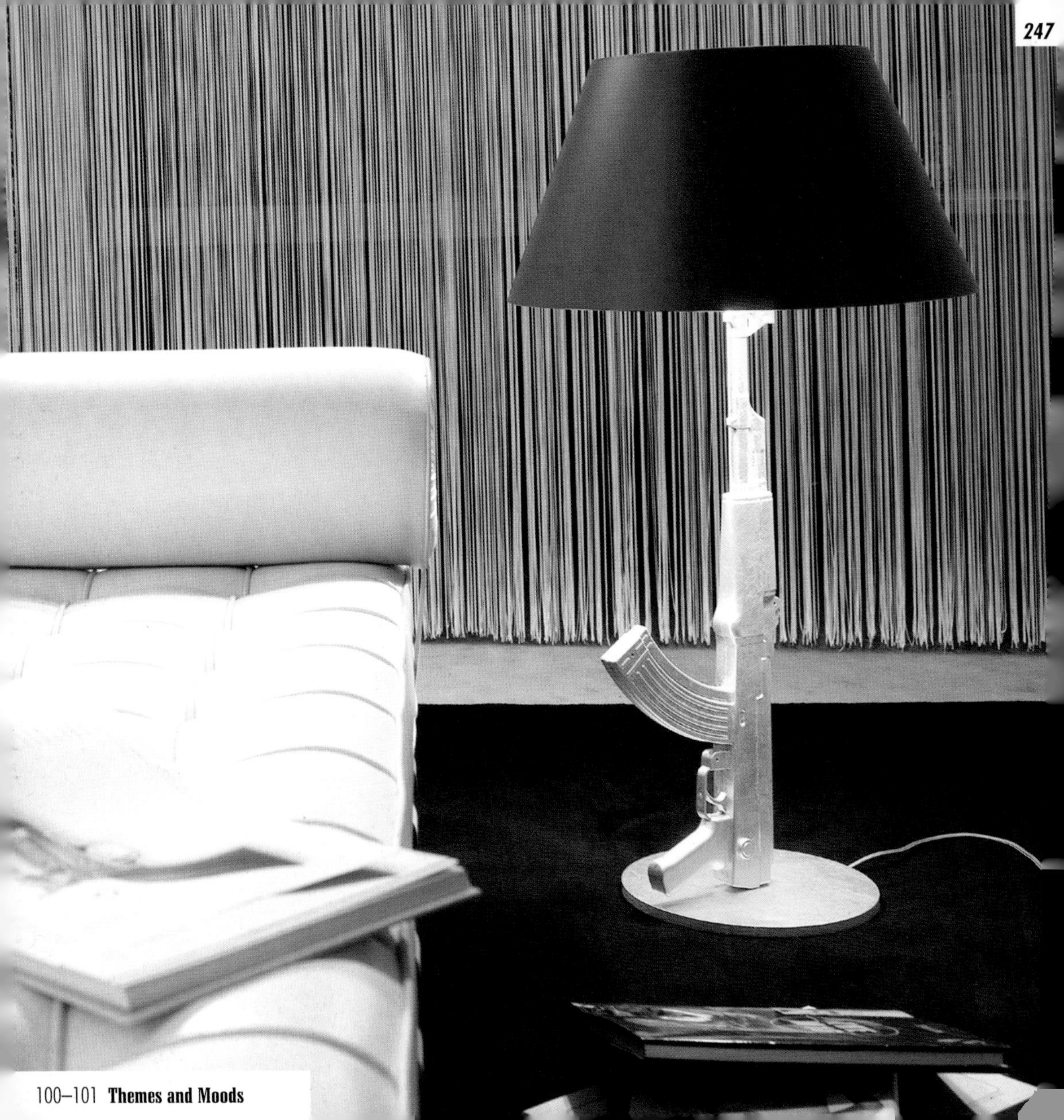

100–101 **Themes and Moods**

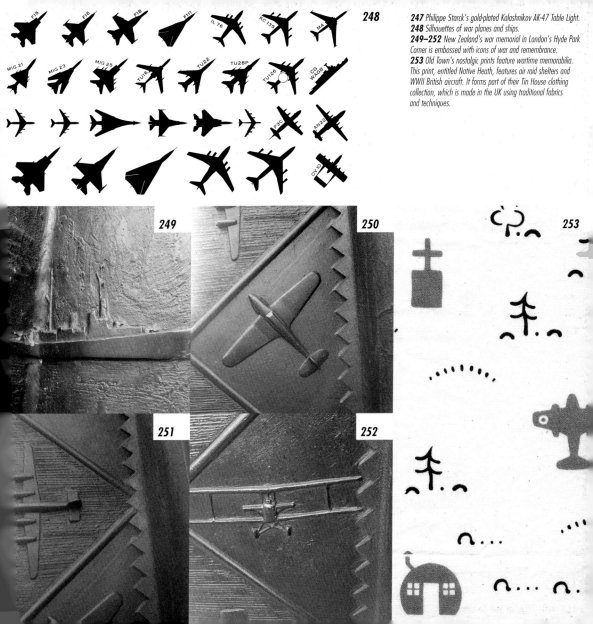

247 Philippe Starck's gold-plated Kalashnikov AK-47 Table Light.
248 Silhouettes of war planes and ships.
249–252 New Zealand's war memorial in London's Hyde Park Corner is embossed with icons of war and remembrance.
253 Old Town's nostalgic prints feature wartime memorabilia. This print, entitled Native Heath, features air raid shelters and WWII British aircraft. It forms part of their Tin House clothing collection, which is made in the UK using traditional fabrics and techniques.

"There has been a lot of pro-war rhetoric here in the States lately; I guess this is my reaction to all that. I am not an overly political person but this idea came to me and I felt the need to express it somehow.

"This is just a series of simple iconic statements on how our government and the US media try to candy-coat what is really happening in Iraq and Afghanistan, and how this administration's idea of liberation seems to come in the form of destruction. Oooh baby, it's a mad world."

Trent Good, for Rollout

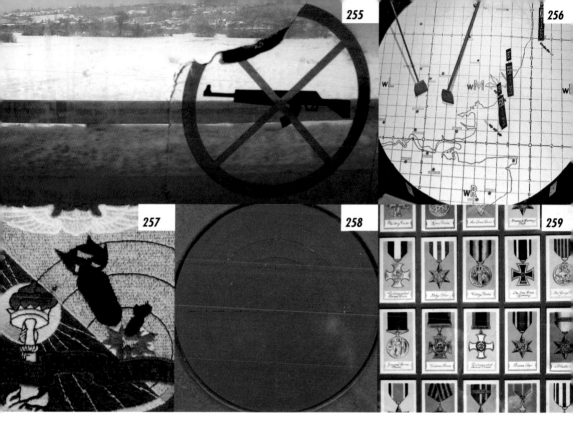

255

256

257

258

259

260

Trent Good's War Babies wallpaper design for Rollout.
255 *No weapons: a view from a Mongolian train window by Jannie Armstrong.*

256 *War time navigational tools, taken by Leo Reynolds.*
257 *Commemorative regimental sew-on patches featuring dropping and exploding bombs.*

258 *Radar chart.*
259 *A selection of medals on collectible cards.*
260 *Medal pictograms.*

"We're wearing black military uniforms that have universal symbols of peace on them. The heart represents love and hope. The cross/first aid represents care and the human spirit. The gold image/abstract of us in gold represents unity"

Tim DeLaughter, The Polyphonic Spree

261 The Polyphonic Spree: "The Fragile Army," photographed by Hal Samples.

262

263

264

26

266

267

268

269

IN
REMEMBRANCE

270

271

262 CND symbol in rainbow colors.
263 John Lennon memorial with the peace symbol in flowers.
264 No Bombs on this Stop the War Coalition banner.
265 Nobel Peace Prize medals.
266 Brooklyn Industries peace dove T-shirt.
267 Flower Power.
268 Chinese symbols for peace.
269 The poppy, symbolic of remembrance.
270 A dove of peace in stained glass.
271 Commemorative poppies on the New Zealand war memorial in London's Hyde Park Corner.
272 A peace banner.
273 A sincere message of peace, truth, simplicity, and equality.

272

273

Peace
和平

PEACE + TRUTH
SIMPLICITY + EQUALITY

...on butterflies.
...ns away in the
...nce near Gaza
...up a constant
...rumble

'After a bowl of

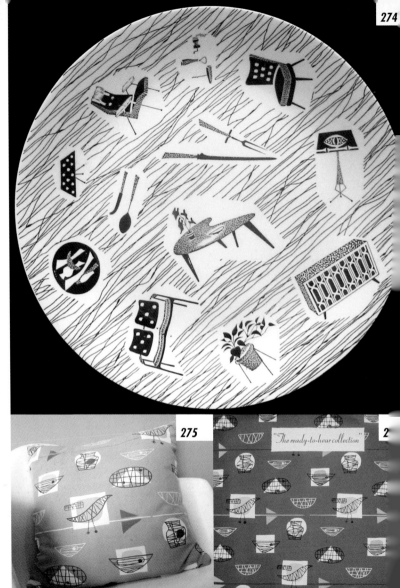

Domestic Symbols

Designed in the 1950s by unknown student Enid Seeney, Woolworths' range of Homemaker crockery was an instant hit. Not only was the form of the individual pieces streamlined and modern, but also the graphic black-and-white pattern featured ultra-modern furnishings of the time, such as Robin Day's reclining chair and Terence Conran's spindly-legged wicker plant-pot stand. The success of Homemaker was largely due to the fact that it appealed to a growing sense of optimism following years of wartime austerity. The psychology is easy to grasp. You may not be able to afford the Robin Day chair itself, but your purchase of the crockery bearing it shows that you are modern and fashionable.

While the crockery displayed symbols of an aspirational contemporary lifestyle, it became symbolic itself of post-war mass-market modernist style, and a society that had started to break down class hierarchies. Not only that, the range helped make icons of some of the mid-century designs it depicts. Its current collectible status belies Homemaker's intended affordability: a soup terrine, originally sold by the thousands for just 12 shillings and sixpence, regularly fetches over £100 at auction today.

274 Enid Seeney's classic Homemaker for Woolworths. The design features a Robin Day chair and, an icon of its time, the kidney-shaped coffee table.
275 1950s textile design by Marian Mahler for David Whitehead features interior products in abstract such as loungers and vases.
276 The Compact Organisation appropriated the Mahler fabric in the early 1980s for record sleeves for their Ready-to-Hear collection.
277 Mini Moderns Sitting Comfortably? wallpaper features various chairs to color-in. Ideal for the younger modern design enthusiast.

"The ready-to-hear collection"

Self-referential domestic motifs have long adorned items of interior furnishing, proving to be an enduring design device. Erica Wakerly's Homes design on wallpaper and fabrics depicts interiors populated with furniture in an eclectic mix of styles. In simple line drawings, this work continues in the tradition of designs by Marian Mahler and, indeed, Homemaker. Meanwhile the cosy interiors of past generations offer inspiration for modern pieces of jewelry by fashion label Comfort Station: quirky items like the cuckoo clock display baroque exuberance and a hint of fantasy.

Suggestive of culinary proficiency, kitchen utensils are a perennial favorite symbol on all kinds of kitchenalia, from dish towels to storage jars. Contemporary designs give an ironic nod to the past, when kitchens would be wallpapered with illustrations of teapots and copper kettles (chosen to represent nostalgic homeliness) or wine labels and spice jars (symbols of epicurean adventurousness).

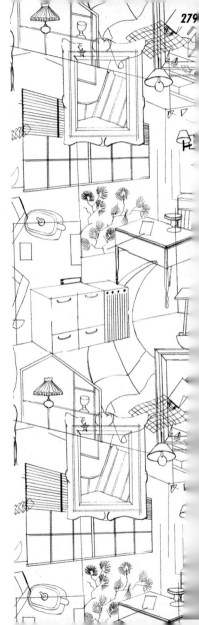

279

278

280

281

278 and 279 This award-winning Homes design by Erica Wakerly is available as a fabric and a wallpaper and continues the trend for referencing interiors on interior products.
280 and 281 Cuckoo clocks as style icons—seen here on the jewelry of Comfort Station.
282 Tick Tock wallpaper by Mini Moderns.

282

283 Hemingway Design took inspiration from prosaic kitchen equipment to create this stylish pattern.

285 The Art of Wallpaper designer Belynda Sharples also used everyday kitchen objects in this Pots and Pans wallpaper design.

284 and 287 Designer Heather Moore of South Africa-based Skinny La Minx created the Borrowed Spoons dish towel design in a serendipitous collaboration with three other design bloggers. After reading Jasper Morrison's "A Book of Spoons," she photographed all the spoons in her house and posted them on her blog, inspiring three other artists to do the same. With the permission of the other three, Heather used the collected images to create the design.

286 The inspirational original: vintage kitchen utensils wallpaper discovered at her grandfather's house by Christi Carlton.

283

284

285

There can be few domestic chores that induce more of a sense of dread than ironing. But in these post-feminist days, when we're all meant to be multitasking domestic divas, the marketing people encourage us to embrace the reality and even the pleasure of everyday tasks. Well, that's the theory, anyway. Some perceptive designers have abstracted the symbols of laundry and cleaning to make witty comments on domesticity. Extracted from their care labels and embossed on ceramic tiles, or printed and woven on fabric, the signs and symbols associated with domestic chores become decorative features—symbols of dread turned into beautiful adornments.

288–290 Designers Pieces of You use domestic wash care symbols in this fabric design.
291–295 Artist Caren Garfen's work focuses on women and the domestic. Her research showed that women are still the principal care takers in the home. She uses silk-screen print and hand stitching to create the pieces entitled Womanual.

288

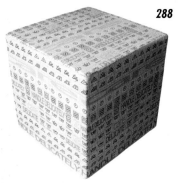

292

293

girl dressed up
as mum, doing all the mothers
chores inc vacuuming, tidying
and washing

woman and daughter using
product

294

295

KFC's Mums Night Off
Bucket

Finish Odour Stop

296–298 *Nita Rege and Bessie Turner of Blink created these Washing Tags ceramic tiles featuring the iron, hand wash, do not bleach, do not tumble dry, and 40° wash symbols.*

299 Top row L/R: 95º machine wash—permanent press; 60º machine wash; 60º machine wash—permanent press; 40º machine wash; 40º machine wash—permanent press.
2nd row L/R: Hand wash; Do not wash; Do not wring; Professionally clean; Professionally dry cleanable in all solvents; Dry cleanable in perchloroethylene, hydrocarbons (heavy benzines).

3rd row L/R: Dry cleanable in perchloroethylene, hydrocarbons (heavy benzines)—with restrictions on addition of water, mechanical, or drying processes; Dry cleanable in hydrocarbons (heavy benzines); Dry cleanable in hydrocarbons (heavy benzines)—with restrictions on addition of water, mechanical, or drying processes; Only oxygen bleach allowed; Do not bleach; Any bleach allowed.

4th row L/R: Chlorine bleach allowed; Iron at low heat; Iron at medium heat; Iron at maximum heat; Steam iron; Do not steam iron.
5th row L/R: Do not iron; Tumble dry at normal setting; Tumble dry at medium heat; Tumble dry using permanent press setting; Do not machine dry.

Transport and Industry

Transport pictograms reduce the car's features to either a front view of headlights and grill, or a boxy side profile. Inevitably, this makes them easy to recognize on road and parking lot signage, but ignores the subtlety of automobile design. The car acts as a barometer of changing design styles. There are periods when sleek rounded edges are in fashion; at other times angles and facets prevail. In addition, certain models have become associated with particular personality types and designers often depict cars not only for their iconic design status but as symbols of these characteristics and associations: the laid-back surfer appeal of a VW Camper or the retro chic of the Citroen DS.

Transport symbols can represent conflicting themes: mankind's progress, summed up by the invention of the internal combustion engine, or the irresponsible pollution of the planet due to selfish over-dependence on personal transport. Depictions of industry similarly refer to power production methods: oil rigs, power pylons, and cooling towers—the things that enable industry—act as more tangible symbols than abstract industrial processes. These symbols align themes of industry with the impervious might of nations and corporations. Meanwhile, personal industry (or Do-It-Yourself) is symbolized through more prosaic tools and components—from drills, hammers, and saws to nuts, bolts, and spigots.

300 Beijing parking lot sign. *301* Keyring for the car keys. *302* Car mechanic symbol. *303 and 305* Car club badges. *304* Stylized car symbol.
306 In her wallpaper design CARS GO BEEP II for Studio Printworks, contemporary artist Jessica Smith combines design texture and motion to create a pattern of choked-up traffic cacophony. Available in both Smog grays and Enviro green colorways.

"The Planes, Trains and Automobiles wallpaper designs appear in The Central Hotel, in Blacktown—adjacent to a busy train station, which influenced the theme.

"The design is a repeat pattern of transport pictograms mixed with food and drink symbols and more abstract ones like a skull and crossbones."

Sophie Tatlow, Deuce Design

307 and 308 The Deuce Design wallpaper in the interior of The Central Hotel in Blacktown, Australia. Photographed by Dean Wilmot.

309 *London Transport by People Will Always Need Plates.*

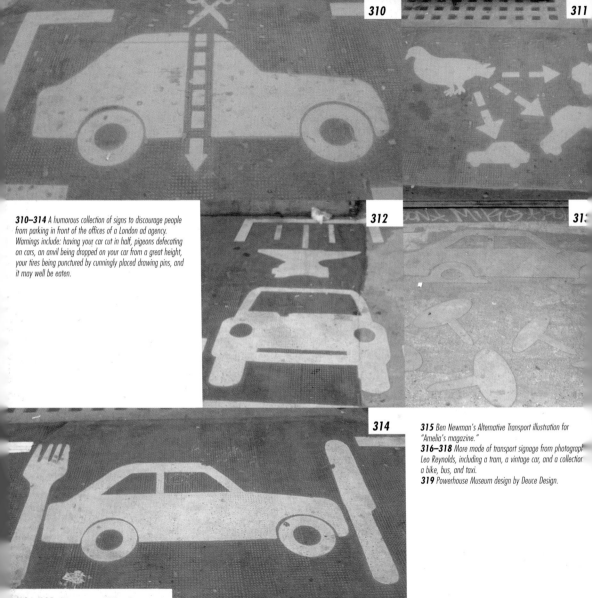

310 | **311**

312 | **313**

310–314 A humorous collection of signs to discourage people from parking in front of the offices of a London ad agency. Warnings include: having your car cut in half, pigeons defecating on cars, an anvil being dropped on your car from a great height, your tires being punctured by cunningly placed drawing pins, and it may well be eaten.

314

315 Ben Newman's Alternative Transport illustration for "Amelia's magazine."
316–318 More mode of transport signage from photograph Leo Reynolds, including a tram, a vintage car, and a collection a bike, bus, and taxi.
319 Powerhouse Museum design by Deuce Design.

315

316 EAST ANGLIA TRANSPORT MUSEUM · CHAPEL RD., CARLTON COLVILLE, LOWESTOFT.

317

318 taxi

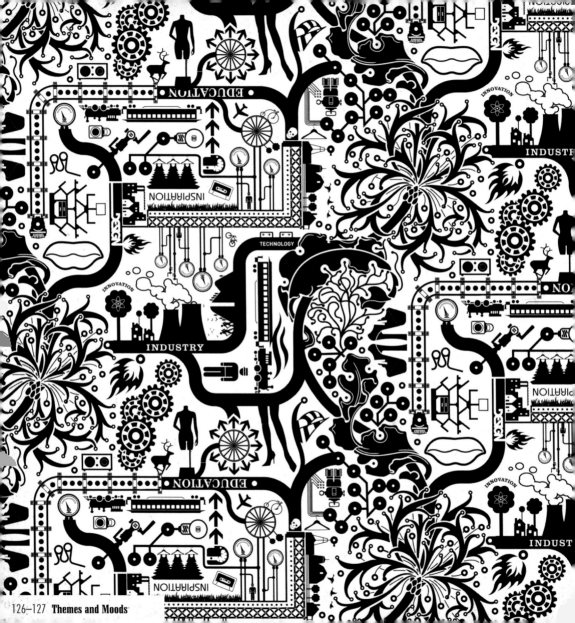

"Yee-Ha! pokes fun at the mythology of Texas cowboys, oil, and football within the structure of a fanciful, rococo damask pattern."

Paul Loebach, for Studio Printworks

320, 322, and 324 Hardware store frontages featuring tools.
321 Icons on a plumber's merchant's truck livery.
323 Mongolian industry immortalized in stained glass—seen here by Jannie Armstrong.
325 More outdoor signage celebrating industrial achievement.
326 Yee-Ha! wallpaper by Brooklyn-based artist Paul Loebach, uses an oil drilling image at its center.

Science and Space

Much of the visual vocabulary of science makes it into the graphic representation of scientific themes. Atomic orbitals and molecular structures are a case in point. These diagrams and 3D models, created to represent the makeup of matter, hold an enduring allure. They were the basis for textile designs and furniture by the great designers of the mid-20th century, like Charles and Ray Eames and George Nelson. Used in art and advertising, these symbols immediately say "science;" they were revisited by Damien Hirst and Jonathan Barnbrook in the concept and graphics for London's Pharmacy restaurant and bar, open between 1999 and 2003.

Science and space travel themes are used in popular culture and communication to suggest that products and services are "cutting edge." From the 1950s onward, companies have invoked orbiting satellites, sputniks, starburst motifs, and satellite dishes to imbue their brands with attributes of dynamism, speed, energy, modernity, and magnetism.

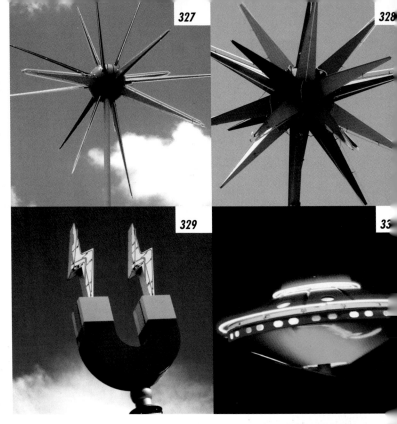

327–330 A selection of scientific 3D icons photographed by Jennifer Remias.
331 and 332 For the cover of David Byrne's "Feelings" album, Stefan Sagmeister commissioned a series of Byrne dolls with different expressions: happy, sad, and angry—juxtaposing these emotions with space-age typography and a starburst.

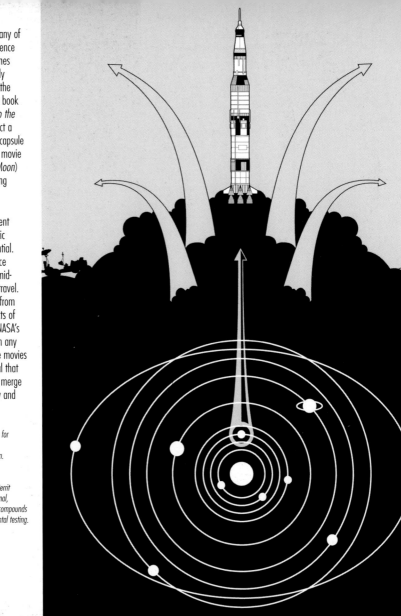

In a curious case of life imitating art, many of the signs and symbols that stand for science and space are based on, or reflect, themes prevalent in science fiction from the early 20th century. Jules Verne is considered the father of science fiction literature. In his book *De la Terre à la Lune* (*From the Earth to the Moon*), scientists and engineers construct a 900-foot-long cannon to shoot a space capsule to the moon. Georges Méliès' prescient movie *Le Voyage dans la Lune* (*A Trip to the Moon*) predates the first successful moon landing by 67 years.

These visions of the future set a precedent for fact and fiction to merge in the public mind. The cycle has become self-referential. Thus, much of the iconography of science and space has changed little since the mid-20th-century pioneering days of space travel. Commemorative space mission badges from the Soviet era now look like the products of a creative director's retro imagination. NASA's logo looks no more or less credible than any number of identities created to promote movies about space travel. And it seems natural that theme parks like Disney's Epcot should merge signs and symbols from both the reality and fiction of science and space.

333 *Rockets limited-edition poster by Brian Flynn for Hybrid design.*
334 *Robot Origin by Brian Flynn for Hybrid design.*
335 *Hydrade Sports Drink distributor brochure designed by Derrit DeRouen for Decoder.*
336 *Cerilliant capabilities brochure designed by Derrit DeRouen for Decoder. As part of Radian International, Cerilliant is a company that synthesizes chemical compounds and comparative samples for drug and environmental testing.*

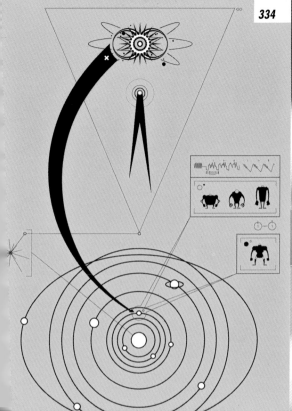

ANALYTICAL REFERENCE MATERIALS & CUSTOM SYNTHESIS AND SERVICES

Cerilliant
Science, Down to a science.

INVIGORATING OPPORTUNITY

...atistics. In the sports drink industry, increasing ...is fueling explosive growth – more than 11.5% ...ast five years. The retail prices of sports drinks ...contrast to those of carbonated soft drinks. ...e market for sports drinks is projected to ...n in retail sales during 2000. A refreshing ...beverage industry? The evidence is conclusive.

... to capture the momentum of this segment, ...ot options. But check the facts first. Make sure

you choose the brand formulated to offer better taste. Certified to deliver superior nutritional value. The only one with a unique ingredient scientifically proven to rehydrate the body faster than any other sports drink in the world. And the industry leader for innovative packaging with an eye-catching, resealable Mylar Pouch.

The truth is, Hydrade features all the things today's active, health-conscious consumers want in a sports drink. And it's clearly the best choice to help you quench your thirst for higher beverage sales and targeted business growth.

THE RESULTS CONSUMERS WANT

Hydrade is the only sports beverage scientifically proven to revitalize and replenish the body faster. The secret? Hydrade's super-hydrating combination of glycerol and electrolytes, which we call Revitalytes™. Research shows this unique formulation actually improves overall conditioning and endurance levels. In fact, these Revitalytes optimize consumers' performance benefits by improving the body's cooling ability, helping to prevent dehydration and delaying the onset of fatigue. With Hydrade, consumers get the only ready-to-drink sports beverage available with glycerol – and they get the real results they expect.

Hydrade
glycerol
active in
scientifica
to revive, r
and rehydr
bod

Hydrade delivers
thirst-quenching
quitability with
four popular
flavors and wildly
exhilarating taste.

THE TASTE CONSUMERS CRAVE

A refreshing change in the sports drink segment, Hydrade features satisfying taste that extinguishes thirst like nothing else. Non-carbe and bursting with flavor, Hydrade allows consumers to enjoy ma. quipability and successfully combat dehydration. So while it is the v most advanced sports drink, Hydrade draws consumers back for

U.S. SPORTS BEVERAGE MARKET

$400 $600 $800 $1000 $1200 $1400 $1600 $1800 $2000
DOLLAR SALES (IN MILLIONS)

The U.S. sports beverage market is projected to top $2 billion in retail sales during 2000 - up from $300 million in 1986. U.S. per capita consumption of sports drinks is up 580% from 1985, while market leaders have successfully maintained a premium pricing policy.

(Source: Beverage Marketing Corporation of New York, 1998)

337 Visible Robot limited-edition poster by Brian Flynn for Hybrid design.
338–340 and 345 From the collection of Richard and Olga Davis, these vintage Soviet badges celebrate satellites and space travel, using simple iconography to ensure the enameled badges clearly communicate their messages.

341 Cut-price rockets?
342 Radiating rings of communication and electricity on this vintage Marconi badge.
343 A shooting star.
344 Simple space and technology icons with a vintage science fiction look.

338

339

341

342

343

344

345

Nature

Floral motifs have long been a staple of the decorative arts. We are used to wallpaper and fabrics adorned with flowers and foliage, but recently a greater diversity of natural signs and symbols have been making their way into the work of artists and designers. Whether inspired by the woodland settings of folk and fairy tales or the archives of natural history museums, what is significant is the abundance of living creatures in the work of these "new naturalists." Butterflies, bees, birds, dragonflies, deer, insects, and fish all feature in illustrative and 3D work suggestive of a romantic escapism and an appreciation of individuality over mass-production—concerns these makers share with their forefathers in the Arts and Crafts movement.

What has changed is the recognition of the role of technology and machinery in producing designs. While the original exponents of Arts and Crafts purposefully turned away from industrialization, current designers positively embrace the juxtaposition of craft and technology: laser cutting is teamed with hand screen printing; computer generated repeat patterns are reproduced on traditional presses that create a hand-blocked effect.

346 Imprint butterfly suede skirt pin by jewelry designer Anna Lewis.
347 Bees wallpaper by Absolute Zero Degrees features honeycombs morphing into bees and butterflies.
348 Spray-painted butterfly icon.
349 Chinese national park signage.
350 and 351 Butterfly icon used to symbolize emerging new design talent in this event branding for Creative Future for the British Council by Mumbai based-designers UMS Design Studio.
352 Moth jewelry design by Comfort Station.

347

348

349

臭椿
Ailanthus altissima
(Mill.) Swingle.

350

BRITISH
COUNCIL

UK | CREATING

creative future

351

352

dance with
me

353

"The 'Cathexis' installation consists of over 3,000 suspended wooden birds embellished with pattern, which swarm en masse throughout the building. It has several layers of symbolic meaning which include prayers and wishes, memories and memorial, superstitions and fragmented narratives. These associations underline a more personal theme of loss and fragility, as 'Cathexis' is also a delicate memorial to my grandmother.

"Cathexis means an attachment or transfer of emotional energy and significance onto and into an object, idea, or person. Memory, memorial, superstitions, amulets, and shrines are interconnecting themes which inspire and inform my work, be it jewelry or large-scale installation. I now realize that I am striving to discover the symbolic significance of objects in people's lives, whether they be personal, religious, cultural, or universal."

Anna Lewis, jewelry designer

353–355 Anna Lewis's "Cathexis" installation at the Mission Gallery in Swansea.

356–358 Trinity Bar wall treatments by Australia-based Deuce Design.
359 Brooklyn Industries Overgrown City T-shirt print.
360 Squires and Company's identity for World Forestry Center.
361 Natural beauty spot signage.
362 Spray-painted symbols of leaves soften an urban environment.
363 Artist Wendy Earle's ceramic wall art featuring birds, leaves, and insects.
364 The Moose bar logo stenciled onto cabin-style wood panels.

359

360

361

362

363

364

BROOKLYN INDUSTRIES

THE MOOSE

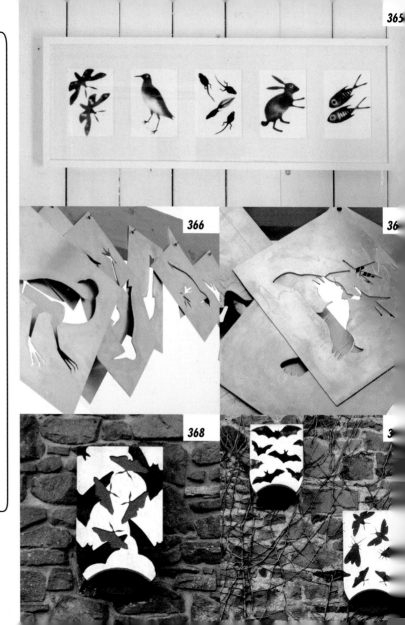

"My work is preoccupied with landscape and wildlife. This is helped by the fact that I live and work in a secluded valley in the west of Wales. The planting of thousands of trees and the reintroduction of wetlands and flowering meadows, has resulted in an increase in the variety of wildlife, therefore widening the scope of my work.

"I set out to make pieces that are vital, work that seems to be illuminated by a sense of the magical, always present in life."

Wendy Earle, artist

365 A framed example of Wendy Earle's bird, insect, and animal studies.
366 and 367 Hanging in the artist's studio are a selection of stencils, hand-cut in steel panels to withstand the heat of a blow torch when creating the work.
368 and 369 Much of Earle's work is intended for the outdoors, such as bird boxes that double up as illuminations by reflecting the winter sun, or as cabinets enshrining images of birds. These bat boxes feature silhouettes of bats and insects and are intended to encourage bats to nest in them. Allowing the passage of time and the effects of natural weathering to alter the pieces is an important aspect of the work.
370–378 A selection of works in Earle's series of bird, insect, and animal studies.

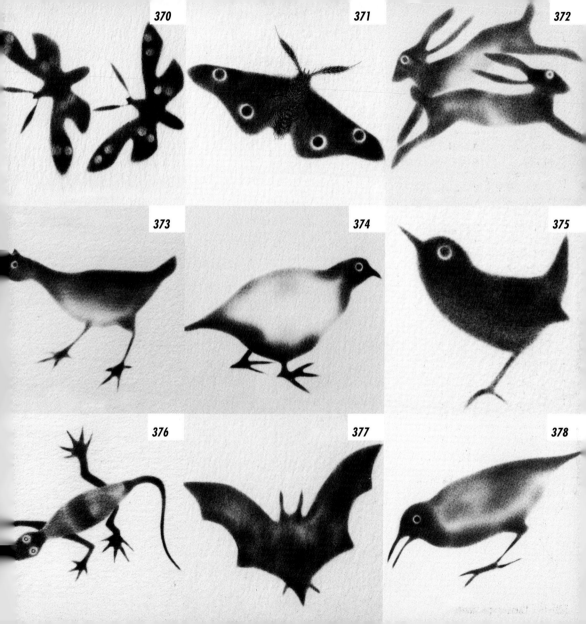

Seasonal

Christmas might be a Christian festival, but its pagan roots are revealed in many of the symbols associated with it. Pagans used to cut boughs of evergreen trees in December, move them into the home or temple, and decorate them to recognize the Winter Solstice, which occurs around the time we now celebrate Christmas. This is the origin of the Christmas tree, one of many evergreens associated with the season. Bright red holly berries were associated with winter magic; ivy was thought to symbolize immortality; mistletoe was said to keep away lightning. It was believed that the cold, sunless winters made evil spirits more powerful. Light and noise were used to drive away spirits—hence the origins of Christmas candles and bells.

Other signs and symbols are a mixture of myth and marketing. The Victorians were largely responsible for many of the rituals we now associate with Christmas, including sending Christmas cards. Father Christmas (or Santa Claus) also evolved at this time from a version of Saint Nicholas of Myra into the figure we know today. Coca-Cola has used Santa Claus in its Christmas advertising since 1931 and popular myth has it that Santa wears a red coat because red is the color of the brand. In fact, while the illustrations of Haddon Sundblom for Coca-Cola cemented his assets (red suit with white trim, black boots and belt, big white beard, red cheeks, fat stomach), Santa appeared in a red coat in illustrations as early as 1870.

379 Ben Newman's poster for an art exhibition.
380 Inseq design's festive toast created by their Zuse matrix toaster.
381 Holiday Coca-Cola packaging design by Hatch, emphasizing the brand's "give, live, love" message. Each variant, including Coca-Cola Classic, Diet Coke, and Coca-Cola Zero has its own individually-created illustrative look.
382 Lorena Barrezueta's limited-edition holiday ceramics.

Signs and symbols help us commemorate the customs and rituals we celebrate throughout the year and thus become associated with the seasons in which they fall. Traditional in the USA and increasingly celebrated in other parts of the world, Halloween is associated with the bright orange of pumpkins that come into season around that time of year, their orange glow redolent of crisp autumnal days.

The Eve of All Saint's Day (November 1st), All Hallows Eve has its origins in the festival of Samhain among the British and Irish Celts. The date marked the end of summer, when land tenures were renewed, and when souls of the dead were thought to return to their homes. Bonfires were lit on hilltops to frighten away evil spirits and eventually a host of witches, hobgoblins, and demons came to be associated with the day.

The origins of the carved pumpkin lantern lie in Irish myth. Stingy Jack tricked the Devil and was banished from Heaven and Hell, destined to roam the earth at night with only a burning coal to light his way. Jack put his burning coal in a hollowed out turnip, earning him the name Jack O' Lantern. Ever since, people have carved similar lanterns with fearsome faces to ward off Jack and other evil spirits on Halloween.

383–389 Icons of Halloween—black cats, pumpkins, witches, carved Jack O' Lanterns, and ghosts.

Food and Drink

Until recently, British pork butchers would frequently advertise their wares with a sign showing a cheery pig wearing a butcher's apron, wielding a meat cleaver. Setting aside the gruesome connotations of a pig that slaughters its own kin, the demise of such signs is an example of how food retail has become increasingly sanitized. In many cases it is sufficient to depict the finished product —a burger, a hot dog, an ice cream—the provenance of the food's ingredients either irrelevant or best unstated. Upscale coffee houses may present themselves by asserting the authentic origins of their coffee beans, while the utensils of food preparation and eating may also be adopted to evoke high culinary standards and an enjoyment of the dining experience.

Food is also an abundant source of symbolism, with fruit particularly rich with metaphorical associations. Citrus fruits are associated with sun and healthiness because of the warm climates they grow in. The apple has biblical connotations of the forbidden fruit. Innuendo ridden bananas and cherries, on the other hand, are both fruits that carry sexual connotations.

390 Pear pillow by Jonathan Adler.
391 Banana pillow by Jonathan Adler.
392 A big orange photographed by Jennifer Remias in Mt. Dora, Florida.
393 Packaging for RDA Organic by Mayday.
394 Fruity gender stereotypes: banana for boys, cherry for the ladies.
395 Signage for Harvey's Groves in Rockledge, Florida.

392

393

RDA
ORGANIC
cranberry, blackcurrant & apple
fresh organic juice

RESTROOMS

394

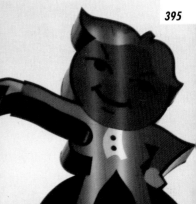

395

396–398 Jennifer Remias has been sign spotting in Florida: Maryland Fried Chicken, Leesburg; Dairy Queen; and Hot Dog Heaven in Orlando.
399 You Are What You Eat identity designed by Lance Wyman in 1960 in his senior year at Pratt Institute.
400–402 Kitchen 24 is a 24-hour modern diner in the heart of Hollywood, with identity and icons by Meat and Potatoes.

YOU ARE WHAT YOU EAT ▶

400

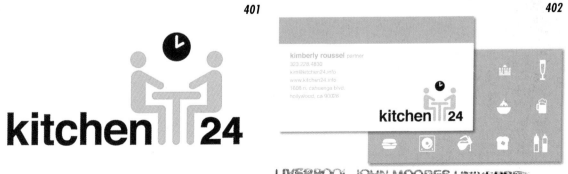

401

402

kitchen 24

kimberly roussel partner
323.228.4830
kim@kitchen24.info
www.kitchen24.info
1608 n. cahuenga blvd.
hollywood, ca 90028

kitchen 24

Find Hidden Foods in the Fall Fores

Many forest mammals store food to eat later, during the lean months of winter. Discover some surprising items in the forest pantry.

Find Hidden Foods in the Fall Forest

Many forest mammals store food to eat later, during the lean months of winter. Discover some surprising items in the forest pantry.

fork
IN THE ROAD

403 Kitchen & Pantry coffee packaging design by Identica, featuring coffee cups growing on the coffee plant to show freshness.
404–405 Exhibition graphics using food utensils in a natural environment by Reich + Petch.
406 A pun gives the design cues for this roadside eatery.

Agriculture

In times of industrialized food production, symbols of agriculture may be invoked to conjure up simpler, more wholesome times gone by: milking and egg collection down on the farm; a horse drawn plough working the fields. Functional agricultural symbols, however, have to ensure safe use of equipment, point out health hazards in times of infection, or promote a company's or even a country's produce in a competitive, increasingly globalized food market.

407 **and** *408* Wheat and Corn Research Center, Mexico. Icons designed by Lance Wyman. *409* **and** *410* Designer Belynda Sharples at The Art of Wallpaper draws on her rural surroundings to create these wallpaper designs. *411* Vintage agriculture and industry icons. *412* Sign featuring the treatment of soil with a pesticide. *413* No bulls or hens—or could this be the symbol The Art of Wallpaper use when they run out of the above wallpaper?

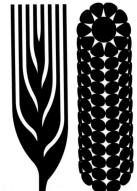

409

410

411

КРАСНОДАР

412

413

414

415

41●

414–419 *A collection of Chinese folk paper-cut designs showing agricultural pursuits.*
420–422 *Images of rural England on these banners photographed by Leo Reynolds.*

417

418

419

中國民间剪纸

CHINESE FOLK PAPER-CUTS

420

421

422

Fortune

A gambler's life is full of meaningful symbols—success or failure can depend on the twist of a card or the throw of the dice. Used in common phrases—"the ace of spades," "the queen of hearts," "lucky seven," "double six"—the symbols of cards and dice are invested with luck and superstition. In popular mythology, the deck of cards is thought to carry metaphysical and astronomical significance: the four suits represent the four seasons, the 13 cards per suit are the 13 phases of the lunar cycle, the 52 cards in a deck symbolic of the number of weeks in a year. Used to represent a rakish life of gambling, playing card suit symbols also carry louche connotations when taken out of a gaming context.

Some lucky signs are more apt for graphic representation than others: the four-leaf clover, lucky star, and horseshoe all succinctly represent themes of luck and fortune. Others require a deeper level of cultural understanding: the watchful eye painted on the prow of Portuguese fishing boats to detect shoals and storms; the Chinese red lantern, raised since the Qing Dynasty to bring luck and prosperity in the New Year. Chinese characters often have dual meanings and Chinese people feel some to be lucky: an upside down Fu sign brings good fortune when posted on a front door, Lu is for prosperity, and Shou brings long life.

423 Luck of the Draw poster by Braley Design, advertising Michael Braley's typography workshop at Iowa State University—which included designing typographic playing cards.
424 Circular King of Spades. .
425 A hand-painted deck of cards.
426 A sign commemorating the iconic Ace cafe in London.
427 Ace and Queen pillows by Jonathan Adler.

Luck of the Draw
Typography Workshop
Iowa State University
College of Design
October 22-23, 2004

Iowa State alum, Michael Braley, will lead a two-day typographic workshop. October 22: 9:00 am–6:00 pm, and Saturday October 23: 9:00 am–6:00 pm. Please contact Angela Griner at agriner@iastate.edu to sign up. Space is limited to twelve students.

Michael Braley is an Art Director in Oakland, California. His work has been recognized nationally and internationally and is in the permanent collections of the San Francisco Museum of Modern Art and the Museum für Kunst und Gewerbe in Hamburg, Germany. Previous to founding Braley Design, Braley was a member of Cahan & Associates, San Francisco, for eight years. He has taught typography at the California College of the Arts (CCA) and has led letterpress workshops at Cal Poly University.

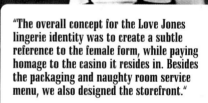

"The overall concept for the Love Jones lingerie identity was to create a subtle reference to the female form, while paying homage to the casino it resides in. Besides the packaging and naughty room service menu, we also designed the storefront."

Todd Gallopo, Meat and Potatoes

428–430 Love Jones identity, packaging, and store interior featuring the icons from the identity, all by Meat and Potatoes.

431

432

433

LUCKY SEVEN · BREAKFAST · BURGERS · SHAKES · BOOTH SERVICE · TAKE OUT

431 Identity for Tom Conran's Lucky Seven restaurant, designed by Nicholas Holbrook.
432 Lucky Seven exterior fin signage.
433 Lucky Seven exterior.
434 A fortune teller fish.
435 In Asia a lucky cat is thought to attract wealth.
436 A red Chinese lantern is a symbol of luck and prosperity.
437 A Japanese pink crane is a symbol of good luck and peace.
438 The eye on Portuguese fishing boats detects shoals and storms.
439 Fortune cookies.
440 A lucky horseshoe.
441 A shooting star.
442 A four-leaf clover.

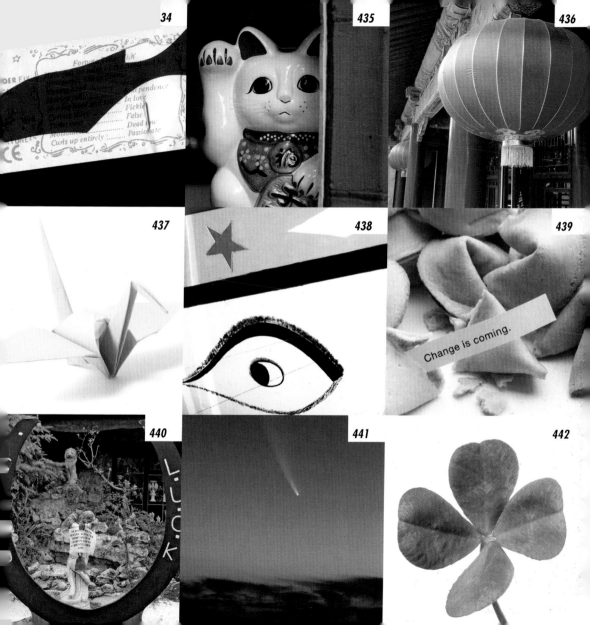

Urban

The built environment offers the creative eye a rich source of signs and symbols that can be used to communicate urban themes. A stencil graffitied image of a homeless person, placard announcing the state of his plight, cup ready to catch spare change from passers-by, seems to sum up the worst aspects of city life.

From Moscow to Tel Aviv, New York to Berlin, urban decay is a popular theme for designers and artists, epitomized by worn flyposter art and street signs bearing the patina of age on concrete and tarmac. But not all symbols of urban landscapes are gritty. Many designers delight in the diverse buildings and architectural details prevalent in the cityscape.

Kensal Rising is a fabric design for St. Jude's by classic British workwear brand, Old Town. Now located in rural Norfolk, England, the designers describe the piece as: "a reference to the fondly remembered Victorian skyline seen from the old North London Railway that runs between Broad Street and Richmond." It features rooftop symbols of chimneys, lampposts, and power lines executed with the charm of 1940s domesticity.

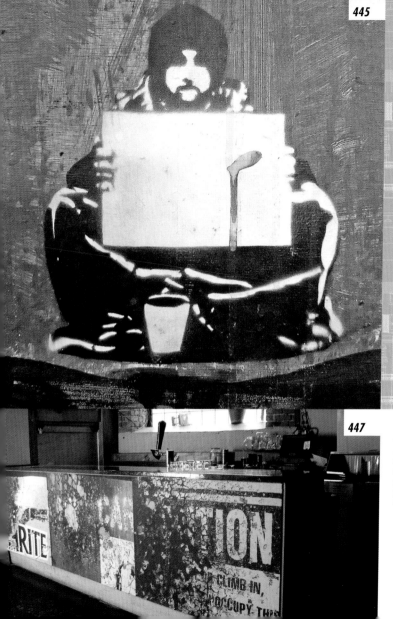

447

443 An urban landscape created by Lo-Tec.
444 Kensal Rising furnishing fabric by Old Town, featuring fixtures of the environment like chimney pots and lampposts.
445 Another fixture of urban living—a beggar.
446 Do you live in a Town? wallpaper by Mini Moderns creates a pattern from an eclectic mix of different buildings from varying periods.
447 Trust wall covering by Sean Orr for Rollout.

Happiness

When State Mutual Life Assurance merged with Guarantee Mutual Company in 1963, employee morale was low. In a move to create what we now call "internal alignment" the company employed graphic artist Harvey Ball to design a symbol to be applied to button badges, desk cards, and posters encouraging staff to smile. The yellow smiley face symbol he created, bearing a resemblance to the Russian Kolobok fairy tale character, has become an international icon. Not originally trademarked, the smiley face fell into the public domain and was popularized by brothers Murray and Bernard Spain, who used it in the early 1970s to sell mugs and bumper stickers with the phrase "Have a nice day." The UK saw a revival of the smiley face as the key symbol of the late 1980s Acid House movement, and the smiley was reappropriated by its creator in 1999 with the creation of the Harvey Ball World Smile Corporation, organizing World Smile Day® to raise money for children's causes with the message: "Do an act of kindness—help one person smile."

Internet culture has further raised the popularity of the smiley in the form of emoticons—typographic symbols made up from punctuation signs. Usually viewed sideways, they range from the straightforward :-) smile, to a cheeky ;-) wink, even an outraged :-@ scream.

448 Leo Reynolds captured this happy face on vacation.
449 The sew-on smiley badge was popular in the 1970s and made a big comeback in late 80s "rave" culture.
450 Up, up, and away...
451–453 More smiley faces seen by Leo Reynolds.
454 These domestic dustpans make any spring clean a happy event.

448

449

4

451
452
453
454

Sport and Activity

From rowing to wrestling, cycling to shooting, there's a pictogram to depict your chosen activity. If you love sport then the plethora of sports and activity signs and symbols will excite and motivate you. If you hate physical activity they will fill you with all the dread of a double gym class. Such is the power of signs and symbols.

Fortunately, you don't have to be athletic to appreciate the sport icons and branding created by Lance Wyman for the 1968 Mexico Olympics—considered by the creative community to be one of the most successfully branded Olympic Games ever. The sport icons were developed based on glyphs found in Mexican pre-Hispanic cultures, tying in with Lance Wyman's logo for the event, which combines the Olympic rings with op-art kinetic typography and traditional forms from Mexican culture. Each icon focuses on an expressive detail, a part of the athlete's body, or a piece of sports equipment. Their clarity is supported by a bold color-coding system, which aided navigation from one event to another.

455–458 Probably the most recognized and well loved Olympics branding—the Mexico 1968 games identity and event icons by Lance Wyman.

456

457

458

Designed in 1913 by Baron Pierre de Coubertin, the founder of the modern Olympic Games, the emblem of the games is composed of five interlocking rings in blue, yellow, black, green, and red on a white field. Upon its initial introduction, de Coubertin stated the following in the August, 1913 edition of *Revue Olympique*: "These five rings represent the five parts of the world which now are won over to Olympism and willing to accept healthy competition." The identity draws upon the symbolism of the ring, standing for continuity and the human being, and has become one of the world's most recognized brands.

If the Olympic Games embody a spirit of fraternity across the global sporting community, one sports brand above all stands for individual achievement. With its dynamic swoosh and "Just Do It" strapline, Nike, named after the Greek goddess of victory, has become synonymous with "personal best" in sport. Its campaigns are innovative and groundbreaking, using a range of signs and symbols to appeal to sub-groups within its broad target audience, while never straying from its core brand values of sports performance.

459 Sailing symbol by Lance Wyman.
460 Logo for postage stamps commemorating the 1970 FIFA World Cup in Mexico by Lance Wyman.
461 Diver says OK! Transfer spotted on an old Italian Vespa.
462 Jorge Jorge created these sport icons for his promotional work for Campos de Férias Desportivas.
463 Part of the Hilton Hotel collection of icons by Lance Wyman and Mark Fuller.

459

461

Campos de Férias Desportivas

462

PORTO
CÂMARA MUNICIPAL

460

464 and 465 To promote the launch of a sport-inspired line of footwear for Nike in boutique retail stores, Hybrid Design create a graphic language that incorporated Nike's sport heritage desig cues and a lifestyle spin on sport apparel and footwear, using ornate graphic elements like old decorative picture frames and custom-designed wallpaper for each store.
Client Art Direction: Heather Amuny-Dey, Art Direction: Dora Drimalas. Design: Dora Drimalas, Caleb Kozlowski. Photography: Jeff Dey.
466 A collection of sporting pictograms.

464

465

466

Skull and Crossbones

Associated with pirates, poison, and religion, the origins of the skull and crossbones symbol are steeped in myth and legend. To the Knights Templar—a medieval Christian military order prominent in the Crusades from the early 1100s until the early 1300s—the sign represented resurrection because of its association with Golgotha, "the place of the skull," site of Jesus Christ's crucifixion. Some crucifixes feature a skull and crossbones beneath the body of Christ in reference to this. Further associations with Christianity come with the Spanish practice of placing real skulls and bones at the entrances of cemeteries.

Death is the prevailing association we have with the symbol—hence its use on bottles and containers to indicate they contain poisonous substances. The practice of marking poison with the skull and crossbones became widespread in the late 19th century and it continues to be the only standard symbol for poison. Its use is, however, becoming less common outside industrial applications since there are concerns that on domestic products the symbol may attract children due to its association with pirates, which youngsters could interpret as a game.

467

468

46

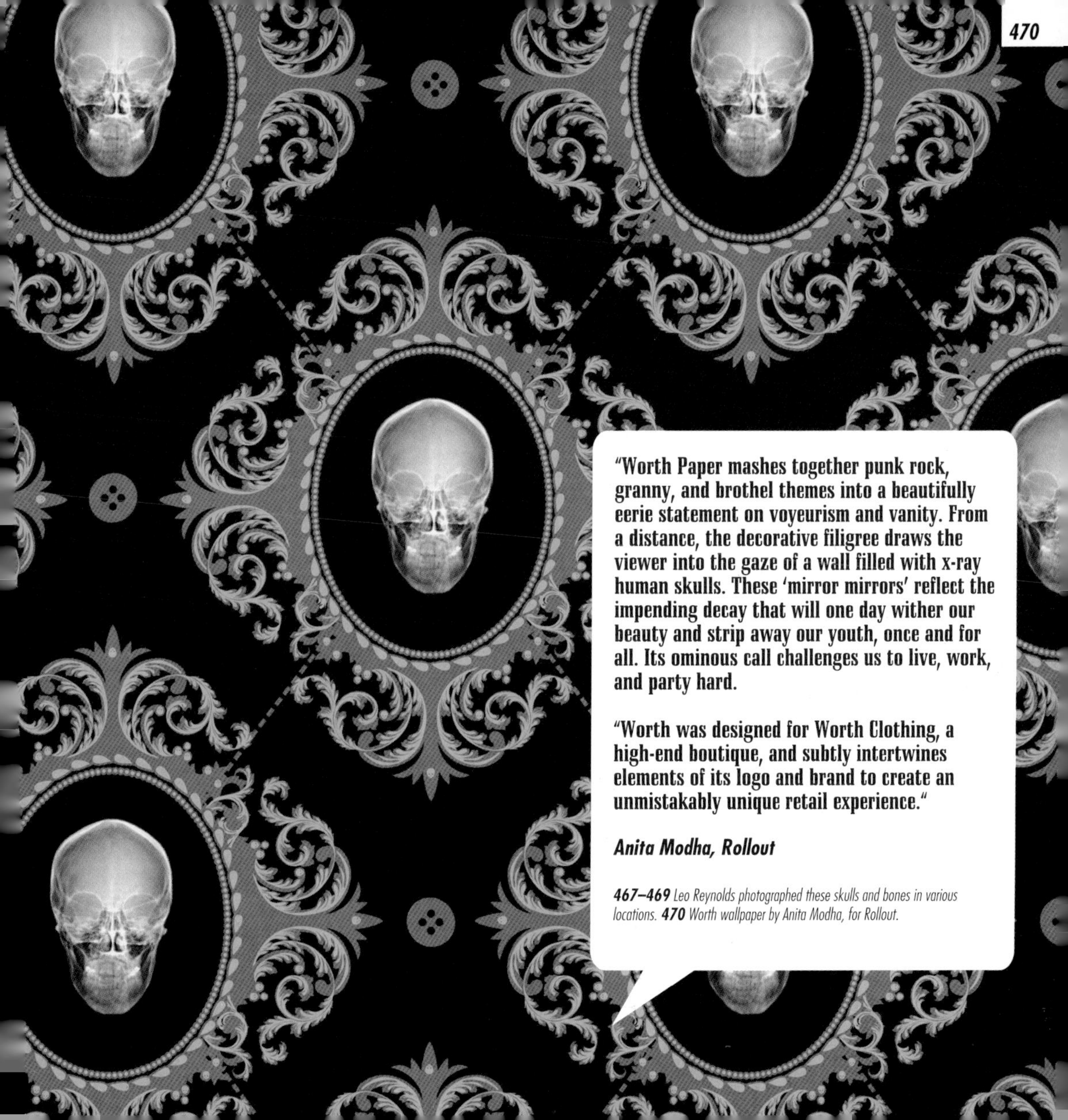

"Worth Paper mashes together punk rock, granny, and brothel themes into a beautifully eerie statement on voyeurism and vanity. From a distance, the decorative filigree draws the viewer into the gaze of a wall filled with x-ray human skulls. These 'mirror mirrors' reflect the impending decay that will one day wither our beauty and strip away our youth, once and for all. Its ominous call challenges us to live, work, and party hard.

"Worth was designed for Worth Clothing, a high-end boutique, and subtly intertwines elements of its logo and brand to create an unmistakably unique retail experience."

Anita Modha, Rollout

467–469 *Leo Reynolds photographed these skulls and bones in various locations.* **470** *Worth wallpaper by Anita Modha, for Rollout.*

471

472

473

474

47

476

TUSESTUDIO.COM

"The Good times are Killing me".

VALENTINE'S EVENING WITH MODEST MOUSE AT THE GROVE OF ANAHEIM IN SUNNY CALIFORNIA

THIS IMMACULATE MESS DESIGNED WITH LOVE BY RIAN AT THEDECODERRING.COM

174–175 **Themes and Moods**

477

478

471–474 and 476 Various skull and crossbones symbols.
475 Modest Mouse Anaheim poster by Christian Helms at Decoder. This "The Good Times are Killing Me" Valentine's night poster features an almost hidden skull in the lipstick traces. From the Modest Mouse 2005 Poster Series, which was a year-long collaborative project with the band producing a unique silk-screened poster to promote and commemorate each live performance. Each poster is based on a specific lyric, allowing fans to purchase posters referencing both the show they attended and their favorite song.
477 Devil or Angel from a range of T-shirts by Meat and Potatoes.
478 A red-eyed Jolly Roger.
479 Poison.
480 Class war sticker seen by Leo Reynolds.
481 Tracy Dobbins gives the skull and crossbones a feminine edge.

479

480

WWW.LONDONCLASSWAR.ORG

481

482

483

484

482–485 *Shazam!* limited-edition art print and T-shirt by Meat and Potatoes. The design incorporates skulls and crossbones in a lightning flash graphic. Its creators urge: "Summon the elders (Solomon, Hercules, Atlas, Zeus, Achilles, and Mercury) with this exciting and dynamic shirt!" Designer: George McWilliams.

The skull and crossbones is most commonly linked with the Jolly Roger—the flag flown by pirates to effect the surrender of a rival ship and its cargo. Some theories link the first pirates with Templars who turned rogue after Papal support was rescinded. The first recorded mention of the Jolly Roger is in the 18th century. The flag was not flown perpetually by pirates at sea; most of the time, they flew no colors so as to go unidentified. They hoisted the Jolly Roger and fired a warning shot as a means of intimidating a target ship. If the target refused to surrender, a red flag was flown, indicating that the pirates intended to take the ship by force.

From Gilbert and Sullivan's *Pirates of Penzance* to the *Pirates of the Caribbean* movies, popular culture has kept pirate legends and the skull and crossbones alive. Various military regiments still use the symbol to assert fearlessness in battle. Versions of the symbol have been used in consumer campaigns to deter video and DVD piracy, home taping, and illegal music file sharing, and these campaigns have, in turn, been pirated and adapted. The symbol appeals to fashion and graphic designers, largely for its rebellious connotations, but also because it is infinitely customizable. Reconfiguring the key elements, replacing the crossed bones or the eyes of the skull with other symbols and icons, invests it with entirely new meanings, while retaining its edgy appeal.

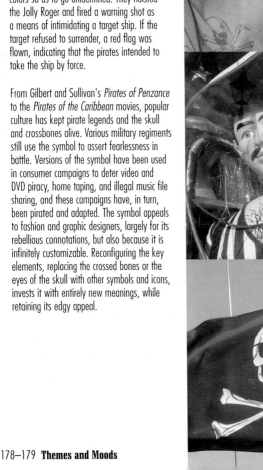
486

487

488

489

ME TAPING IS KILLING MUS...

AND IT'S ILLEGAL

DRM IS KILLING MUSIC

AND IT'S A RIP OFF!

OME SEWING IS
ILLING FASHION

AND IT'S ILLEGAL

The Pirate Bay

486 *Fluorescent skull and crossbones give this blouse an edgy look.*
487 *A fancy dress pirate.*
488 *A skull and crossbones pirate flag, seen here on the beach at Camber Sands.*
489 *Kilo Kai rum logo and packaging by Turner Duckworth adds a touch of wit and style to the skull and crossbones symbol by crafting two K's to form the skull's teeth and bones.*
Creative Directors: David Turner and Bruce Duckworth.
Design Director: Shawn Rosenberger.
Designers: David Turner and Tanawat Pisanuwongse.

490 *Home Taping Is Killing Music icon from the1980s anti-copyright infringement campaign by the British Phonographic Industry.*
491 *Image for the campaign against Digital Rights Management (DRM).*
492 *Home Sewing is Killing Fashion by Bo Peterson.*
493 *The skull and crossbones design cross-reference continues: Pirate Bay logo incorporating the tape cassette and crossbones on its sail.*

Eclectic Icons

Sometimes a single symbol isn't enough. An early 21st-century predilection for decorative over minimalist styles has led to an eclectic mix of signs, symbols, icons, and illustrations being used in applied pattern, textiles, graphics, advertising, and art. This riot of symbols fits broadly within the "maximalist" style identified in the book *Maximalism* by Charlotte Rivers. In her introduction she states: "silhouette and botanical motifs are taking over from rigorous, simple lines and muted tones. A profusion of color and luxury, brimming with excess, is stating the case for a return to sensuality."

Design featuring a mix of clashing icons and symbols can be exuberant, fantastical, playfully nostalgic, or sharply urban. Sourced from street signs, Victorian picture books, and games compendia, the symbols chosen and the medium they are applied to are important, but the magic lies in unexpected juxtapositions: a skull with a martini glass, a rook and a candelabrum, a pail and a pearl necklace. Like visual word association where the logic has flown out the window, this is symbol use at its most abstract, surreal, and fun.

496

498

501

494 and 495 *Two pillows from Jonathan Adler's collage collection.*

496–502 *Assemblage shelving system by Seletti. Each of the 10 wooden crate style boxes is printed with a different silk-screen pattern. The boxes nest inside each other and can be stacked and held together by straps to create a shelf, or can be used separately as small side tables or storage units. Available from Do Shop in London.*

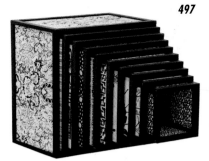
497

499

500

502

503

504

505

506

182–183 **Themes and Moods**

503, 505, and 506 Mixing chess pieces with elaborate candelabra and cameo silhouettes, Comfort Station create jewelry using an eclectic range of iconography.

504 Designer Claire Bradshaw showcases her textile work—itself a carefully selected mishmash of influences and styles—with this self-promotional work that includes different icons, images, and techniques.

507 Michael Browers describes his Isoglyphics typeface as a parody of contemporary society. Featuring a whole range of pictograms and developed as an homage to Otto Neurath, his Isoglyphics represent the "imperfect, broken, and crashed... modern life as a train wreck."

508 and 509 Deuce Design's promotional gift cards are covered in found pictograms mixed with bespoke pattern designs.

508

509

"In my work I put nature and culture together to construct empty atmospheres that dislocate and totemize their subjects. Using digital and manual processes I explore the relationship between loss and creation, memory, technology, and nature.

"The symbols and cards in Pelmonism were originally created for an exhibition at VPCream Artes in Lisbon, Portugal. Visually exploring the temporal nature of objects we attach memory to, and of recollection itself, the designs are incorporated into recognition puzzles and games."

Emily Clay, artist

510–512 Pelmonism is based on the card memory game Pairs. In the work, artist Emily Clay uses symbols of everyday objects to explore themes of memory and sentimental attachment.

Pelmonism

Signals and Information

Music
Typography
Media and Technology
Prohibited
Wayfinding
Sign Language
Road Signs
Health and Safety
Weather Conditions
Recycling

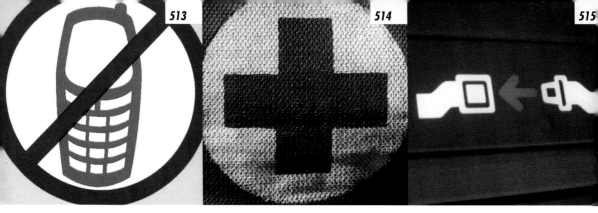

Signals and Information

Signs and symbols are synonymous with the communication of signals and information. Many of the signs featured here reflect everyday life: road signs and wayfinding systems make life more efficient; weather forecasts and health and safety signs help us manage risk. Some information symbols are unavoidable in modern life: a planet simultaneously in the grip of a technological boom and ecological calamity sees technology and media symbols proliferate alongside conservation and recycling signs.

In this chapter we also examine the symbols that have been conveying information for centuries. Typographic symbols are essential for clear and precise linguistic communication, while manual sign language and the symbology of musical notation are codes understood only by the initiated.

513 No cellphones.
514 The Red Cross symbol.
515 Fasten your safety belt, it's going to be a bumpy ride.
516 UK tourist attraction road signage.
517 Any questions?
518 Words Spoken Quieter Than Actions wallpaper by Chloe Perron for Rollout.
519 Information point.
520 Arrow's the name of the hotel and the arrow marks the spot—photo by Jennifer Remias.
521 Old sheet music.
522 Today it will be cloudy with sunny spells.
523 A selection of US road signs.
524 Medical pictogram by Ravi Poovaiah.

5

Music

While the symbology of musical notation is familiar to all of us, only a gifted few can actually understand and follow it. The evolution of modern musical notation and its associated symbols has combined separate systems of indicating pitch and rhythm. Italian Benedictine monk, Guido D'Arezzo placed letters on individual lines to indicate their pitch. These letters evolved into the clef signs used today. Guido also invented a system of naming scale degrees using the initial syllables of the lines of a Latin hymn (ut, re, mi, fa, sol, la), used as names for the six tones, C to A. An additional syllable, ti, was added, and eventually ut was replaced by the more singable do, forming the basis of Rodgers and Hammerstein's iconic song a millennium later. The evolution of the rhythmic notation used today took much longer than that for pitch. Mensural notation, in which each note has a specific time value, assumed its present form during the baroque period.

Crotchets, quavers, minims, and treble clef symbols all serve as graphic shorthand for music, animating a static scene with the suggestion of a tune, a whistle, a hum, even a car horn. Instruments themselves, in silhouette or detailed illustration, can evoke different styles of music. A violin's f-shaped resonance holes have all the finesse of classical music, a saxophone instantly communicates jazz, and acoustic guitars capture the warmth of folk music.

525 *PortalPlayer identity by Michael Braley.*
526 *A music fan with a treble clef tattoo.*
527 *The music for one of Elvis' big hits.*
528 *Soviet era commemorative badge.*
529 *Music shop logo*
530 *Engraved minims.*
531 *Carl Fischer music publishers in New York.*
532 *Bach sheet music.*
533 *Music shop signage.*

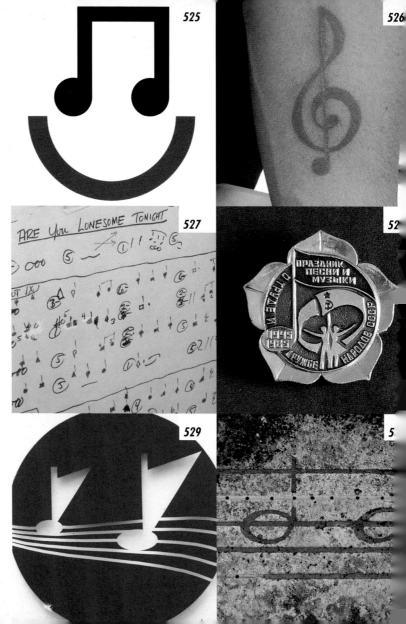

531

532

533

535

537

538

539

540

534 Plinki-Ma-Linki illustration by Ben Newman.
535 Musical notes: treble or G clef, semiquaver, quaver, crotchet, minim, semibreve.
536 Musical annotations: bass or F clef, sharp, flat, natural.
537–539 Design project for the Cairo Opera House featuring musical notation by Hanna Schulz, Silke Muszynski, and Esther Bruna at the Münster University of Applied Sciences.
540 Musical rests: long, breve, semibreve, minim, crotchet, quaver, semiquaver.

1 The shape of the grand piano is the basis for the
lltifunctional Concerto Table by Lovegrove and Repucci.
table has an iPod dock, so it provides both dining surface
dinner party background music at once.
2–546 London design agency CDT created the Sounds
ritain set of stamps for Royal Mail, highlighting the rich
ribution world music has made to Britain's cultural diversity,
ing to break down barriers and unify society. Each stamp
the forms of instruments, players, and dancers to evoke
rent musical genres.
3 Designed by Ocky Murray at Cog Design, the poster for
2007 London Jazz Festival features silhouettes of musical
uments to indicate the musical breadth and diversity of the
am. Also featured is the identity for BBC Radio 3, made
om elements of musical notation.

546

BBC RADIO 3
90–93FM
in association with

LONDON JAZZ FESTIVAL

Friday 16 – Sunday 25
November 2007
londonjazzfestival.org.uk
bbc.co.uk/radio3

Festival Partners

548 US branding and design consultancy JHI created a new identity to mark the 67th National Folk Festival, and bagged an award from the Richmond Ad Club.

549 The following year JHI continued the illustrative theme, featuring folk instruments for an authentic feel on the collectible commemorative poster for the 68th National Folk Festival. Awards came their way again: the poster won the 2007 AIGA award for Best of Posters.

550 A folk guitar morphs into a tree in Absolute Zero Degrees' print for UK fashion brand Fenchurch.

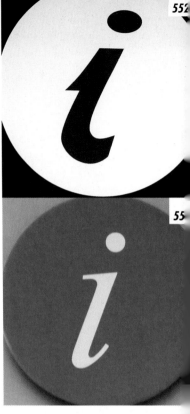

Typography

While words convey meaning, punctuation helps to make sense of the words. These typographic symbols act like tiny graphic sign posts in a sentence, indicating to the reader when to pause and how long for, differentiating between a statement and a question, and offering clues to the correct tonal inflection.

Some typographic signs and symbols have acquired specific communication roles or have been appropriated for applications that make them useful in their own right. The "i" of "information" is frequently isolated to stand as a graphic symbol for any information point. Due to the syntax of email communication, the @ sign has become universally recognized, and is often used to lend a subject hi-tech associations.

→

551 The Burgiss Group is a supplier of investment database products and services. In Lance Wyman's identity for the group, the information "i" icon is used to link the Burgiss signature to products, services, and statements.

552, 553, and 555 Various information signs employing different fonts for the distinctive "i," all captured by photographer Leo Reynolds.

554 Hirschmann Design's identity for Kiosk Information Systems neatly incorporates the information "i" with the "k" of Kiosk.

act:onaid

556 The identity for charity ActionAid, created by CDT, incorporates an inverted "i" that becomes an exclamation mark, creating a sense of urgency and adding punch to the message: "act now!"
557 The exclamation mark features on this hand-drawn attention sign.
558 The symbols say it all: a telephone enquiry point.
559 This stencil graffiti rat's existential angst is summed up by a question mark on a placard.
560 The ubiquitous "at" sign.
561 Decoder's logo for What's Your Vine?—a company specializing in wine-themed apparel and related products.

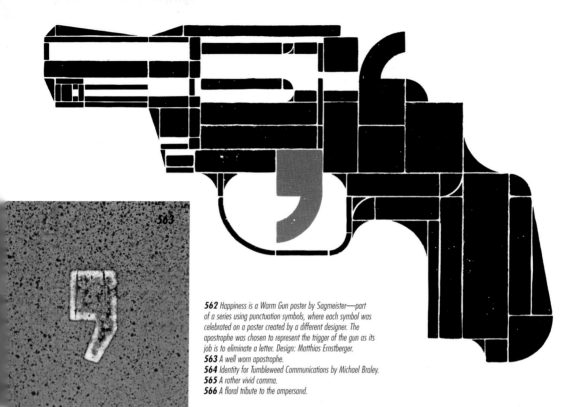

562 Happiness is a Warm Gun poster by Sagmeister—part of a series using punctuation symbols, where each symbol was celebrated on a poster created by a different designer. The apostrophe was chosen to represent the trigger of the gun as its job is to eliminate a letter. Design: Matthias Ernstberger.
563 A well worn apostrophe.
564 Identity for Tumbleweed Communications by Michael Braley.
565 A rather vivid comma.
566 A floral tribute to the ampersand.

euromedia

PRANCER BY KIERAN

RUDOLPH BY NEXTBIGTHING

567 and 568 You can count on design agency Nextbigthing to send innovative, eye-catching, and beautifully designed Christmas cards. For this one, each member of the team created a different reindeer from Santa's herd, using typographic elements in abstract to form the antlers, eyes, and nose. Only Rudolph gets a red nose.

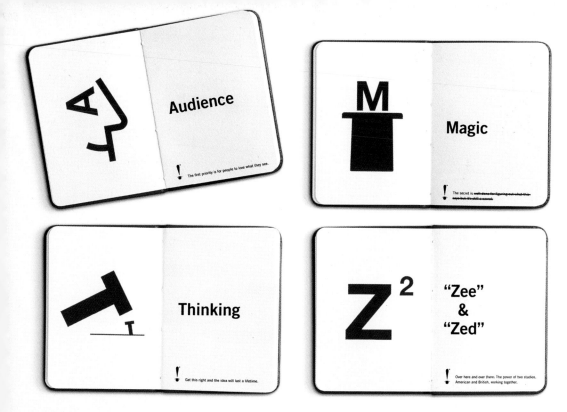

Audience

! The first priority is for people to love what they see.

Magic

! The secret is ~~walk done for figuring out what their says but it's still a secret.~~

Thinking

! Get this right and the idea will last a lifetime.

Z^2 "Zee" & "Zed"

! Over here and over there: The power of two studios, American and British, working together.

9 and 570 *Typographic elements feature in Turner Duckworth's identity and also in the design of* ir *"A–Z of Design" book—a compilation of the principles the consultancy use in their work. They* ·cribe it as a "guide to what makes us tick." It is used as a giveaway for clients and potential clients. ative Directors: *David Turner and Bruce Duckworth.* ·igners: *David Turner, Bruce Duckworth, Anthony Biles, Christian Eager.* ·duction: *Jaleen Francois.*

This book belongs to:

Paula Carson

From:
Bruce Duckworth
020 8994 7190
Bruce@TurnerDuckworth.co.uk

→ Certain typographic symbols are incorporated into communication design and identities to imply an added layer of meaning. An inverted "i" becomes an exclamation mark, imbuing a word with a sense of urgency and import; a strategically placed question mark invokes an inquisitive attitude. Thus, typographic devices help to convey emotion as well as information. Conversely, the actual meaning of letters and typographic symbols can be ignored and instead used playfully as abstract design elements, appreciated for their beauty or graphical usefulness, independent of their meaning.

The notion of dialogue is succinctly conveyed either by inverted commas or the more casual speech bubble. Inverted commas have a formality that lends a sense of gravitas to a piece of communication—suggesting the statement or quote is worthy of chronicling. Speech bubbles are associated with the modern comic book, but they can be traced back as far as the 13th century, when speech scrolls were used as a device to ascribe statements to the subjects of works of art. Modern speech bubbles are extremely versatile: additional information about the nature of the statement can be conveyed according to their shape, including scream, thought, broadcast, whisper, even emotion, when used in conjunction with color.

Don't Tell On Me

Michael Braley
Greensboro, NC
Ad Club of the Triad
October 27, 2004

The Ad Club of the Triad invites you to join us for Michael Braley's lecture
title," Wednesday, October 27, 2004. The lecture will begin at 7:00 p.m.
at 6:00 p.m.) at the Caroline Theatre, Renaissance Room, 310 South
Greensboro. Braley will illustrate the design process by revealing some of his
own. Visit www.adclubofthetriad.com, for more information. Braley is based
in Oakland, California. His work has been recognized nationally and
and is in the permanent collections of the San Francisco Museum
the Chicago Athenaeum of Art and Design, and the Museum für Kunst
in Hamburg, Germany. Previous to founding Braley Design, he was
Cahan & Associates, San Francisco, for eight years. He has taught at
California College of the Arts (CCA), and lectured at several uni...

"Words Spoken Quieter Than Actions is a playful means to allow people to interact with their interiors and to leave a little reminder of themselves. With the comical form of the word bubble, people can express either random or profound thoughts, much like graffiti. By leaving anonymous or specific notes—even back and forth conversations—the wallpaper becomes a collage of whimsical, intelligent, or often silly souvenirs."

Chloe Perron, for Rollout

571 Poster by Michael Braley announcing his lecture to the Ad Club of the Triad. The lecture was a behind-the-scenes look at how design gets produced and how mistakes are often made along the way.
572 Words Spoken Quieter Than Actions wallpaper by Chloe Perron for Rollout allows users to customize their walls with their own comments.

Media and Technology

Including media and technology in a book like this comes with inherent risk. The signs and symbols employed to convey technical information are subject to the same built-in obsolescence as the technologies they represent, as users of SyQuest, Laserdisc, or 8-track cartridge cassettes will testify.

The proprietors of new technologies develop symbols for two reasons: to brand the intellectual property of the technology, and to indicate a device's compatibility with that technology. Since an ever-wider range of technologies is being converged into single multipurpose devices, current media symbols reflect the trend toward this convergence. What we value are options: with separate technologies able to share resources and interact with each other, we seek the reassuring symbols on devices to confirm that a connection can be made via, say, USB or Bluetooth.

There are some symbols that have displayed surprising longevity. We continue to fast-forward, rewind, play, and record well into the 21st century, following the same symbols as ever to do so. Examples of symbols that have survived a fundamental change in technology are camera icons. Despite the rapid shift from film to digital, the basic functions of the camera remain the same. Cameras still carry the enduring symbols to indicate light conditions, portrait, landscape, or close-up, but these have been joined by symbols relevant to digital functionality such as video mode, anti-shake, and red-eye reduction settings.

573

574

575

57◄

577

573 Podcast icon, used in internet transmission.
574 Wireless technology icon.
575 Transfer data technology icon (USB).
576 Transfer data technology icon (Firewire).
577 Feed or RSS icon, used in association with open web syndication formats such as RSS and Atom.
578 A selection of media icons.

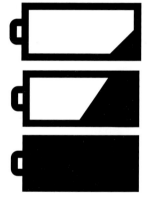

579 A selection of photography icons, including ones to indicate distance, light conditions, and aperture settings.
580 Identity by Lance Wyman for Galeria Fotonauta.

Prohibited

If it feels like modern society prohibits more than it allows, it could be down to the proliferation of the familiar red circle with a diagonal line through it. The sign was originally created as part of road signs to signify a prohibited maneuver (no right turn, no waiting) but is now appropriated by authorities and individuals to prohibit all kinds of undesirable activity—some more reasonable than others.

In short, the red circle and diagonal line are shorthand for "no." No dogs on the beach, no photography in the gallery, no smoking in the cab: the symbol is internationally recognized and, crucially, eliminates potentially unintelligible language. The red, white, and black coloring is rarely deviated from, offering maximum contrast and standout.

581 *Life's a beach—but not for dogs in this seaside location.*
582 *Don't eat apples.*
583 *Don't practice any wheel-based leisure activities.*
584 *US designer Josh Owen created the "Don't" ashtray for Kikkerland based on the familiar prohibited icon. It discourages the smoker while providing a receptacle for ash.*
585 *Don't fish.*
586 *Don't board the tram.*
587 *Don't feed the birds or animals.*
588 *Don't take photographs.*
589 *Don't park here because you'll be towed away.*

EAST R
OF YORKSHIRE COL

N DOGS ON BEACH
1st MAY - 30th SEPT
MAXIMUM PENALTY £50

582

5

584

585

586

587

588

ENLÈVEMENT DEMANDÉ

589

0 The familiar prohibited sign used to drive home a ~~worthwhile~~ social message. Seen here by Leo Reynolds.

◄ A selection of signs used in the public domain either ~~pro~~hibit undesirable activities or to protect the safety ~~of th~~e individual.

Changing

Car Park
Broadcasting
Kitchen Staff Changing
Facilities Management

Wayfinding

The term "wayfinding" generally refers to orientation
and path finding within the built environment.
From museums to sports arenas, hospitals to arts
complexes, effectively implemented wayfinding
systems enhance the user experience. The term was
first coined in 1960 by urban planner Kevin A. Lynch.
In his book, *The Image of the City*, he asserted that
people navigate by forming mental maps based on
five key elements: paths, edges, districts, nodes,
and landmarks.

In 1984 environmental psychologist Romedi
Passini broadened the remit of wayfinding to
include signage and other graphic communication,
sensory information (particularly sound and touch),
space-planning best practice, and provision for
special-needs users. These considerations are all
fundamental to any modern wayfinding brief,
with many consultancies specializing in the
analysis, masterplanning, and implementation
of such systems.   →

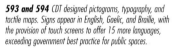

92 UK design consultancy CDT won the Sign Design Society's wayfinding Information Design Award for their wayfinding system for the Scottish Parliament in Edinburgh, which balances accessibility, functionality, quality, and aesthetic principles.

593 and 594 CDT designed pictograms, typography, and tactile maps. Signs appear in English, Gaelic, and Braille, with the provision of touch screens to offer 15 more languages, exceeding government best practice for public spaces.

595–597 The Scottish Parliament wayfinding system creates a clear delineation between public areas, spaces occupied by the politicians, and the functional aspects below ground.

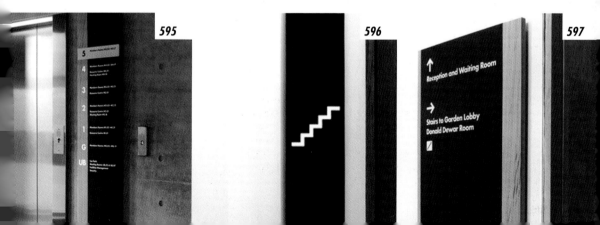

598

599

598–604 Lance Wyman's wayfinding system for the American Museum of Natural History, New York. Each floor of the museum is identified by an icon which is a synthesis of the floor number and the exhibit content. Wayfinding signs and directories combine the icons with photos and floor map panels. The panels are removable for easy updating.

605 and 606 Also by Lance Wyman, each of the Minnesota Zoo exhibit areas is identified by a number combined with an important resident of the area. "Guide Bird" arrows on wayfinding signs guide visitors around the zoo.

600

601

602

603

60

607 由此下山
Way down The Commune

608 大通铺
Shared House

609 石头场院
Rock Field

610 三号别墅
"See" and
"Seen" House

611 家俱屋
Furniture
House

612 怪院子
Distorted
Courtyard
House

613 土宅
Split House

614 森林小屋
Forest House

615 由此上山
Way up the Great Wall

飞机场

"Airport"

607–616 Commune by the Great Wall in the Shuiguan Valley outside Beijing is a private collection of contemporary architecture, designed by 12 notable Asian architects. Each of the houses is available to rent, and the site is open to the public—hence each house has signage in Chinese and English to help international visitors find their way around and identify the individual houses. It is also possible to access the Great Wall from the site by following the arrow signs.

→ Wayfinding systems incorporate icons and pictograms, graphic and written information, and color-coding schemes in an orientation system that has psychological, economic, and safety implications for public buildings and spaces. A well-designed wayfinding system can reduce hospital patients' stress levels, aid efficient business practice, and ensure safe crowd management.

Graphic treatments of icons can be tailored to the purpose and content of a building, enhancing the branding and identity of a space. These considerations aside, at the heart of wayfinding is the requirement to give clear and simple directions, which makes the arrow its hero symbol. Arrows, or pointers, have been used to indicate directions since long before the science of wayfinding was conceived. They can be simple line drawings or elaborate affairs incorporating decorative heads and fletchings. A recent graphic revival has been the pointing hand arrow, its friendly ushering gesture redolent of Victorian poster art.

623

624

617 Makeshift wayfinding: a hand-drawn arrow.
618 This signage incorporates an arrow in the style of a weighing dial.
619 Stylish French directional signage in blue enamel.
620 A hand-carved arrow on a nature trail.
621, 623, and 624 Elegant arrows with elaborate fletchings.
622 Turner Duckworth's design for chef Scott Howard's restaurant incorporates a stylized carrot which reflects his obsession with obtaining the very best seasonal ingredients. It also acts as a visual pointer, directing the public toward the restaurant from the sidewalk.
Creative Directors: David Turner and Bruce Duckworth.
Designers: David Turner and Jonathan Warner.

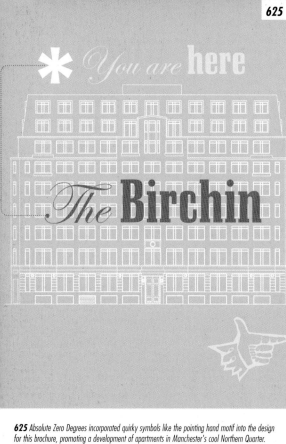

625

626
62

625 Absolute Zero Degrees incorporated quirky symbols like the pointing hand motif into the design for this brochure, promoting a development of apartments in Manchester's cool Northern Quarter.
626 Jonathan Adler's J'Accuse pillows point the finger in genteel needlepoint.
627 and 630 The pointing hand sign has a friendly ushering gesture and a nostalgic feel.
628 A chunky retro arrow seen in Antwerp.
629 A plank of wood is easily crafted to create an arrow, as seen in Beijing's fashionable Dashanzi art district.
631 This sign, seen on the streets of Moscow, uses a broken arrow that seems to point to something round the corner.

Sign Language

The Spanish cleric Juan Pablo Bonet is credited with setting out the first methodology of using manual signs for educating the deaf and improving both the verbal and the nonverbal communications skills of deaf-mutes. Sign language uses a combination of manual gestures to represent the individual letters of the alphabet (allowing words to be spelled out), and gestures that represent objects, activities, and ideas. The letter signs are also used to create shorthand gestures to represent words—for instance, in British Sign Language Monday is communicated by signing the letter "m" twice.

It's often assumed that sign languages are a translation of and therefore dependent on oral language: a gesticulated version of the spoken word. But sign language is independent of the spoken word and develops in its own right. This is borne out by the anomaly that even countries that share a spoken language do not necessarily share a signed language: British and American sign languages are quite different and mutually unintelligible. In fact there are nearly as many versions of signed language as there are spoken languages. Because it doesn't share the linear constraints of the spoken word, many ideas and concepts can be incorporated into signing at the same time. This expressiveness is exploited in the growing art of signed poetry—where the use of gestures adds another dimension to the meaning that words alone could not.

632 *The American Sign Language alphabet uses one hand.*
633 *The British Sign Language alphabet uses two hands.*

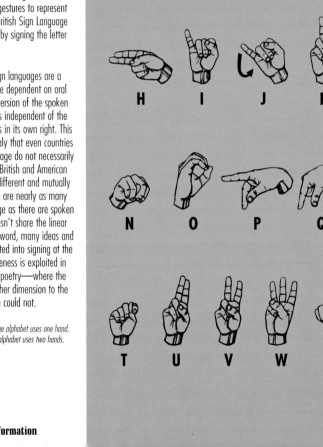

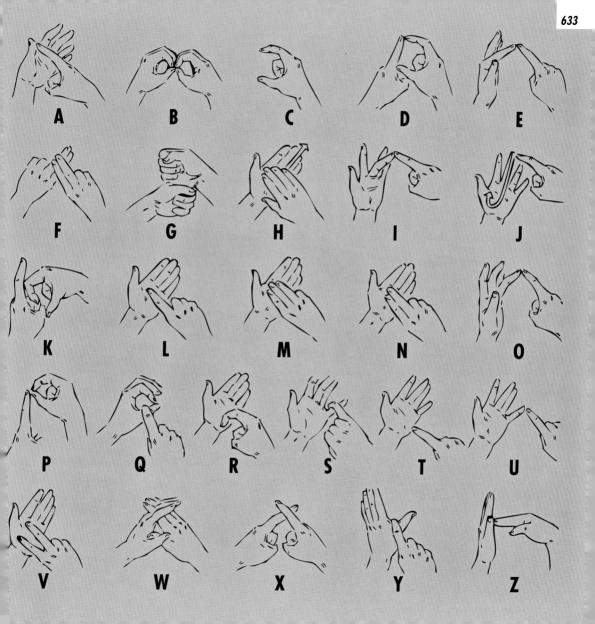

Road Signs

Driving in foreign countries can be a bewildering experience, not least because of the requirement to quickly familiarize oneself with a new set of road sings. Thankfully, there are enough shared conventions in terms of color coding and symbols to offer some consistency.

Nonetheless, local conventions can be visually disorientating. The USA employs the widest variety of shapes in its signage: triangles for yield signs, circles for railroad advance warning signs, octagons for stop signs, pentagons for school advance warning signs, diamonds for warning signs, trapezoids for recreational area guide signs, and pennants for no passing zone signs. Then there is a wide range of route marker shapes, usually in the distinctive shield shape. The USA also allows a degree of latitude from state to state on road signs—every state and province has different markers for its own highways, but use standard ones for all federal highways. Some special highways such as Historic US 66 have unique signs.   →

634 US road signage employs more shapes than other countries—seen here are shields in various colors used for route markers, the octagonal stop sign, the pentagon for school advance warning signs, and the brown recreational sign.
635 An octagonal stop sign in South Beach, Miami.
636–638 Commissioned by London agency Out Of The Blue, this campaign at the Glastonbury Festival combines road signage with slogans based on dance music tracks and bespoke illustrations by Absolute Zero Degrees to discourage driving under the influence of drugs.

→ Perhaps the most significant overhaul of road signage was the development of a consistent system for Britain's roads and motorways from the late 1950s to the mid 1960s by graphic designers Jock Kinneir and Margaret Calvert. Full of post-war optimism, the pair replaced a confusing mishmash of road signs with a coherent system of lettering, colors, shapes, and symbols. They developed a new typeface, Transport, which was a refinement of Aksidenz Grotesk, designed to be friendlier than the blunt modernist lettering used on continental European road signs. The European use of pictograms was adopted, and Calvert devised many of the symbols by drawing on aspects of her own life: the cow featured in the "farm animals on the road" warning sign was based on Patience, a cow on her relatives' farm. Still in use today, the system stands as a role model for modern road signage. Margaret Calvert asserts that the simple communication of information was the essence of the brief: "Style never came into it. You were driving toward the absolute essence. How could we reduce the appearance to make the maximum sense and minimum cost?"

Brown road signs with white icons are for recreational and cultural interest use. They are sited by the roadside to direct visitors to their intended tourist destination toward the end of their journey. The color coding of these signs clearly distinguishes them from standard directional signs. A wide variety of symbols are used on these signs, illustrating different types of attraction or facility: from fairground to nature reserve, Roman fortress to vintage car museum.

639 A selection of British tourist attraction signs.

"Michael Pinsky, curator of the Lost O, thrives in his art on giving subversive new meanings to objects he discovers on site. Preferring to reframe them rather than add to the world's clutter, he has gathered a disparate collection of road signs made redundant by the Shared Space project. Uprooted from their original roadside functions, these assorted signs appear stubbornly upright and even vigilant. Their fronts still insist on warning us to 'Give Way,' announce the 'End of Cycle Route,' and proclaim the advent of a 'Cul De Sac.' But viewed from behind, they reveal metal backs as bare and purged as the most uncompromising abstract sculpture."

Richard Cork, art critic

640–645 The Lost O was a program of temporary public art created to celebrate Breaking Boundaries, an innovative scheme led by Kent County Council to replace Ashford's one-way ring road (hence, the Lost O) with a pedestrian and motorist "shared space." Michael Pinsky's installation seen here was one of a number of works by international artists.

Health and Safety

A number of symbols are associated with medicine and its related professions. A symbol of wisdom, immortality, and healing in Middle and Far Eastern cultures, the snake particularly features in pharmaceutical symbols. Widely known is the serpent of Epidaurus on the staff of Aesculapius, which appears on the crest of the Royal Pharmaceutical Society of Great Britain. Aesculapius was one of the Greek gods of medicine, and is usually depicted carrying a staff with a snake coiled around it. A common variation is the serpent with the bowl of Hygeia, Aesculapius's daughter and a Greek goddess of health. Other variations include the Caduceus, two snakes on a staff, popular for use as a general medical symbol, and the serpent around a palm tree symbol used by French and Portuguese pharmaceutical bodies.

Tools of the trade also feature, such as the carboy, a glass vessel with a bulbous base tapering to a narrow neck, commonly displayed in pharmacy shop windows filled with brightly colored liquids, and the pestle and mortar, sometimes combined with the "Rx" sign which appears at the start of prescriptions. Universally acknowledged to stand for the Latin word "recipe" meaning, "take thou," it has also been suggested that this relates to the astronomical sign of the planet Jupiter. →

646–648, 650, 658, and 659 The red cross was replaced by the green cross in the early 20th century.
649 Identity for medical catheter technology company, Cathcare, by Hirschmann Design.
651 The serpent with the bowl of Hygeia.
652 and 655 The pestle and mortar with Rx sign.
653 Identity by Hirschmann Design for Boulder Associates—specialist healthcare architects.
654 The serpent of Epidaurus on the staff of Aesculapius.
656 Carboys used to be displayed in pharmacists' windows.
657 and 660 Medical pictograms designed for Indian public hospitals by Ravi Poovaiah.

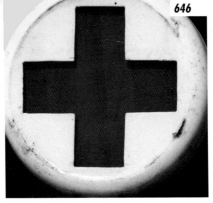

646

647

First aid

648

649

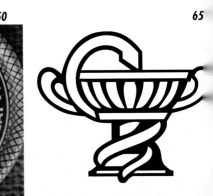

650

65

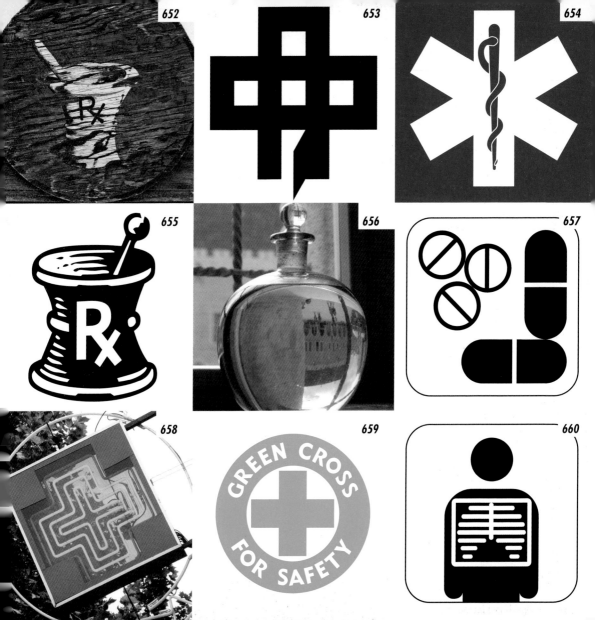

→ Most familiar today, the green cross was first introduced as a pharmaceutical symbol in continental Europe in the early 20th century as a replacement for the red cross, which had been adopted by the International Red Cross in 1863, necessitating the need for an alternative.

It is a legal requirement to display information and action symbols in work and public places. Their design is regulated by the ISO—the International Organization for Standardization—and color coding plays an important role. Red is used for information signs related to general safety or fire safety signs, which convey equipment location, egress, permitted actions, and fire equipment location.

A blue surround shape is required on all ISO-compliant mandatory action symbols. Most frequently seen in industrial workplaces or at the entrance to construction sites, these are the signs that convey precautions that should be taken to avoid hazards, such as wearing protective clothing, deploying safety guards, or washing hands.

661 Fire extinguishers carry vital safety information in the form of signs and symbols.
662 A selection of red color-coded fire safety signs.

663 ISO-compliant mandatory action signs have a blue surround. They are commonly seen in the workplace or at the entrace to construction sites.
664 A sign indicating the mandatory wearing of protective glasses—with additions from a member of the workforce.

Weather Conditions

In the complicated business of weather forecasting, reliable observations and accurate data constitute essential "tools of the trade." These observations, recorded by weather stations around the world, are plotted using a system of 100 "present weather symbols" developed by the World Meteorological Organization. The symbols facilitate extremely detailed observations to be simplified into a codified system offering information about the type, time, and severity of the conditions being observed. The information is accurate to the past hour, so a clear idea can be gained of whether a condition is intensifying or abating.

Luckily, when it comes to conveying the weather forecast to the general public, the symbols become much more straightforward. We get an idea of what's in store through icons that represent tangible conditions: sun, rain, snow, cloud, wind. Because they are universally understood, these symbols have taken on associations beyond their meteorological role. For instance, protective clothing manufacturers may use similar symbols to indicate a garment's level of protection in adverse conditions. So it's easy to see the extremities of temperature against which your coat will protect you, or the windproof rating of your tent.

665 *Simple weather symbols sum up the forecast for the general public.*

666 *In total the Met Office has 100 codes for recording the current weather at the time of the observation:*

1st row, L/R *Cloud development not observed or observable / Clouds dissolving or becoming less developed / State of sky on the whole unchanged / Clouds generally forming or developing / Visibility reduced by smoke haze / Haze / Widespread dust in suspension in the air, not raised by wind at or near station at the time of observation / Dust or sand raised by the wind at or near the station at time of the observation, but no well-developed dust whirl(s), and no sandstorm seen: or, in the case of ships, blowing spray at the station / Well-developed dust whirl(s) or sand whirl(s) seen at or near the station during the preceding hour or at the time of observation, but no duststorm and sandstorm / Duststorm or sandstorm within sight at the time of observation, or at the station during the preceding hour.*

2nd row, L/R *Mist / Patches of shallow fog or ice fog/ More or less continuous shallow fog or ice fog less than 2m on land or 10m at sea / Lightning seen, no thunder heard / Precipitation within sight, not reaching the ground or surface of sea / Precipitation within sight, reaching ground or the surface of the sea, but distant, i.e. estimated to be more than 5km from the station / Precipitation within sight, reaching the ground or surface of the sea, near to, but not at the station / Thunderstorm, but no precipitation at time of observation / Squalls at or within sight of station during the preceding hour or at time of observation / Funnel cloud(s) at or within sight of station during the preceding hour or at time of observation.*

3rd row, L/R *Drizzle (not freezing) or snow grains, not falling as showers / Rain (not freezing), not falling as showers / Snow, not falling as showers / Rain and snow or ice pellets, not falling as showers / Freezing drizzle or freezing rain, not falling as showers / Shower(s) of rain / Shower(s) of snow, or of rain and snow / Shower(s) of hail, or rain and hail / Fog or ice fog / Thunderstorm (with or without precipitation).*

4th row, L/R *Slight or moderate duststorm or sandstorm, has decreased during preceding hour / Slight or moderate duststorm or sandstorm, no appreciable change during preceding hour / Slight or moderate duststorm or sandstorm, has begun or increased during preceding hour / Severe duststorm or sandstorm, has decreased during preceding hour / Severe duststorm or sandstorm, no appreciable change during preceding hour / Severe duststorm or sandstorm, has begun or increased during preceding hour / Slight or moderate drifting snow, generally low (below eye level) / Heavy drifting snow, generally low (below eye level) / Slight or moderate drifting snow, generally high (above eye level) / Heavy drifting snow, generally high (above eye level).*

5th row, L/R *Fog or ice fog at a distance at time of observation, but not at the station during preceding hour, the fog or ice fog extending to a level above that of the observer / Fog or ice fog in patches / Fog or ice fog, sky visible, has become thinner during preceding hour / Fog or ice fog, sky obscured, has become thinner during preceding hour / Fog or ice fog, sky visible, no appreciable change during preceding hour / Fog or ice fog, sky obscured, no appreciable change during preceding hour / Fog or ice fog, sky visible, has begun or has become thicker during preceding hour / Fog or ice fog, sky obscured, has begun or has become thicker during preceding hour / Fog o. ice fog, sky visible / Fog or ice fog, sky obscured.*

6th row, L/R *Drizzle, not freezing, intermittent, slight at time of observation / Drizzle, not freezing, continuous, slight at time of observation / Drizzle, not freezing, intermittent, moderate at time of observation / Drizzle, not freezing, continuous, moderate at time of observation / Drizzle, not freezing, intermittent, heavy (dense) at time of observation / Drizzle, not freezing, continuous, heavy (dense) at time of observation / Drizzle, freezing, slight / Drizzle, freezing, moderate or heavy (dense) / Drizzle and rain, slight / Drizzle and rain, moderate or heavy.*

7th row, L/R *Rain, not freezing, intermittent, slight at time of observation / Rain, not freezing, continuous, slight at time of observation / Rain, not freezing, intermittent, moderate at time of observation / Rain, not freezing, continuous, moderate at time of observation / Rain, not freezing, intermittent, heavy at time of observation / Rain, not freezing, continuous, heavy at time of observation / Rain, freezing, slight / Rain, freezing, moderate or heavy / Rain or drizzle and snow, slight / Rain o. drizzle and snow, moderate or heavy.*

665

8th row, L/R *Intermittent fall of snowflakes, slight at time of observation / Continuous fall of snowflakes, slight at time of observation / Intermittent fall of snowflakes, moderate at time of observation / Continuous fall of snowflakes, moderate at time of observation / Intermittent fall of snowflakes, heavy at time of observation / Continuous fall of snowflakes, heavy at time of observation / Diamond dust (with or without fog) / Snow grains (with or without fog)/ Isolated star-like snow crystals (with or without fog) / Ice pellets.*

9th row, L/R *Rain shower(s), slight / Rain shower(s), moderate or heavy / Rain shower(s), violent / Shower(s) of rain and snow mixed, slight / Shower(s) of rain and snow mixed, moderate or heavy / Snow shower(s), slight / Snow shower(s), moderate or heavy / Shower(s) of snow pellets or small hail, with or without rain or rain and snow mixed, slight / Shower(s) of snow pellets or small hail, with or without rain or rain and snow mixed, moderate or heavy / Shower(s) of hail, with or without rain or rain and snow mixed, not associated with thunder, slight.*

10th row, L/R *Shower(s) of hail, with or without rain or rain and snow mixed, not associated with thunder, moderate or heavy / Slight rain at time of observation / Moderate or heavy rain at time of observation / Slight snow, or rain and snow mixed, or hail at time of observation / Moderate or heavy snow, or rain and snow mixed, or hail at time of observation / Thunderstorm, slight or moderate, without hail but with rain and or snow at time of observation / Thunderstorm, slight or moderate, with hail at time of observation / Thunderstorm, heavy, without hail but with rain and or snow at time of observation / Thunderstorm combined with duststorm or sandstorm at time of observation / Thunderstorm, heavy, with hail at time of observation.*

667

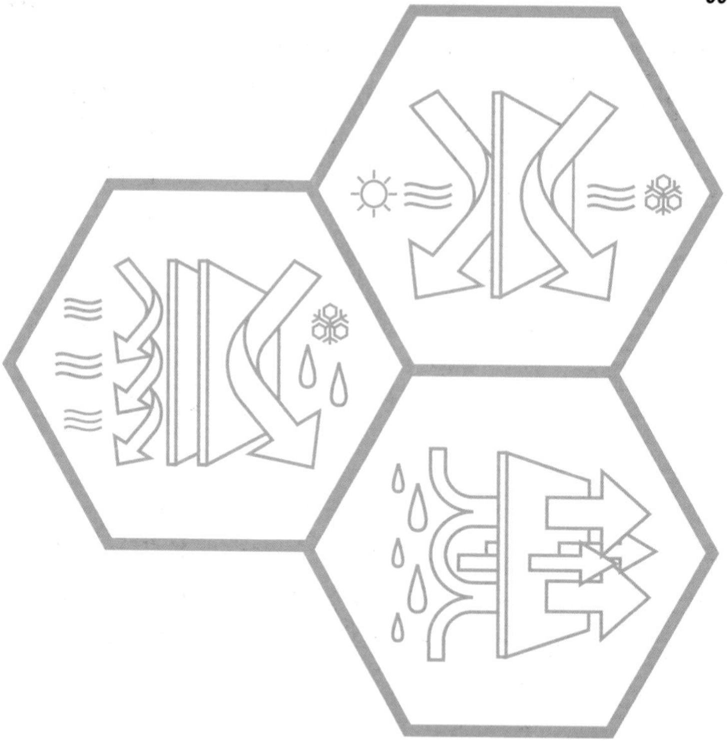

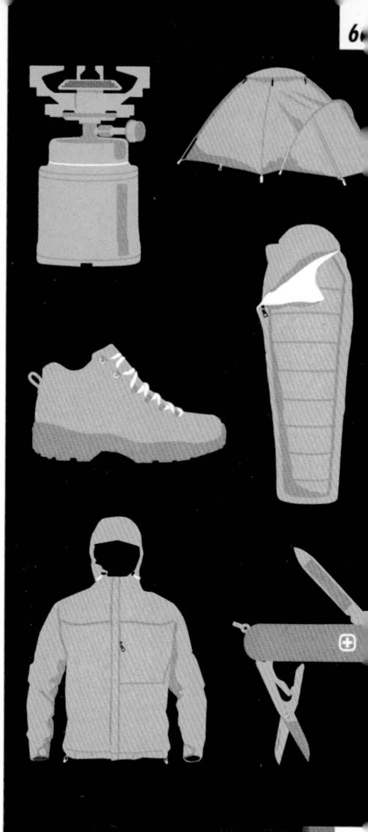

667 Weather condition signs are often used to emphasize a product's performance. These symbols, designed by Brian Flynn at Hybrid Design for Nike F.I.T. Technologies highlight: Dri-F.I.T., Storm-F.I.T., and Therma-F.I.T.
668–671 These icons, designed by Dalziel + Pow for outdoor product retailer Blacks are used in retail as department identifiers and on products to highlight performance specifications.

669

KIDS

WOMEN'S
PERFORMANCE JACKETS

EXTRA PROOFING	**DON'T FORGET**	**WATERPROOF RATING** HIGH	**RING AND PIN SYSTEM**	**NO SEE UV MESH**	**WINDPROOF RATING** HIGH
PROTECTION STEEL TOECAP	**OPTIMAL USE** 2 WALKING	**BREATHABILITY** HIGH	**ADJUSTABLE BACK SYSTEM**	**SUN PROTECTION FACTOR** 30+	**ADJUSTABLE BACK SYSTEM**
WEIGHT LIGHTWEIGHT	**COLDPROOF RATING** VERY COLD	**HYDRATION COMPATIBLE**	**CAPACITY** 25 LITRES	**RIPSTOP FABRIC**	**TAPED SEAMS**
PACK SIZE 38cm x 19cm	**EXTREME TEMPERATURE** -10 °C	**COMFORT TEMPERATURE** -5°C to +10°C	**AIRFLOW BACK SYSTEM**	**CAPACITY** 10	**INFORMATION**
COLOUR CODED POLES	**ANTI-BUG TREATMENT**	**FIRE RETARDANT** FR	**ANTI-BACTERIAL TREATMENT** AB	**INTERNAL LIGHTING**	**RAIN COVER**

672 A selection of vector snowflake icons

673 "Nitin:Snow" is a coffee-table book designed by US agency konnectDesign to showcase photographer Nitin's series of images shot in snowy Vancouver. The tactile Nytek Novasuede cover is embossed with Nitin's logo in a snowflake configuration

674 JHI collaborated with illustrator James Kraus to develop a set of icons that act as banners for the range of products and services offered by a company that manufactures weather-sensing devices. Clockwise from top left: Freeze-Clik (temperature), Mini-Clik (rain), Customer Service, and Wind-Clik (wind).

Recycling

Set to become the sign of the century, the recycling symbol sums up modern eco anxiety. Its history can be traced back to the first Earth Day of 1970, when recycled paperboard producer, the Container Corporation of America set a contest for art and design students to create a symbol that would raise awareness of environmental issues. The winner was Gary Anderson and his design of three arrows forming a Möbius strip is now the universal recycling symbol.

The symbol is not a trademark and any legitimate recycled goods are free to carry it. Many variations are used by local and national organizations to promote individual recycling schemes. One of the most widely recognized in Europe is Der Grüne Punkt (the Green Dot), which indicates that the manufacturer of the product has signed up to an agreement to contribute to the cost of recovering and recycling its packaging.

675–677, 679, and 682 *A selection of Chinese recycling and water conservation signs.*
678, 680, 681, and 684–686 *Bottle and can banks and recycling bins carry a number of variants of recycling signs—each developed by individual initiatives. In addition, signs give instructions to the public to ensure recycling is properly sorted.*
683 *Packaging that carries the symbol of Der Grüne Punkt (the Green Dot), reassures the user that the manufacturer of the product will contribute to the cost of recovering and recycling its packaging.*
687 *Various eco symbols.*
688 *Gary Anderson's original 1970 recycling symbol is not a trademark and can be used on any legitimate application.*

681

Containers

All containers must be emptied, rinsed with caps discarded.

ble-Top artons

aerosol cans

metal cans

drink boxes

glass bottles & jars

green
brown
clear

plastic bottles & jars

1 and 2

only

682

其它垃圾
Other waste

683

DER GRÜNE PUNKT

684

recycle
for London

685

Cans & Metal

350ml

686

SERVE AU VERRE

Appendix

Index

Contributors

Featured Designers and Suppliers

2Fresh
www.2fresh.com

Absolute Zero°
www.absolutezerodegrees.com

Anna Lewis
www.annalewisjewellery.co.uk

Ben Newman
www.bennewman.co.uk

Blink
www.blinktiles.co.uk

Brooklyn Industries
www.brooklynindustries.com

Cabin Project for Motherbrand
www.motherbrand.com

Caren Garfen
caren.garfen@btconnect.com

CDT
www.cdt-design.co.uk

Claire Bradshaw
claire_844@hotmail.com

Cog Design
www.cogdesign.com

Comfort Station
www.comfortstation.co.uk

Dalziel + Pow
www.dalziel-pow.co.uk

Deuce
www.deucedesign.com.au

Do
www.do-shop.com

Emily Clay
www.pelmonism.com

Erica Wakerly
www.printpattern.com

Esther Bruna, Silke Muszynski, and Hanna Schulz
nurfuerhanna@gmx.de
silke.muszynski@gmx.de
esther_bruna@web.de

Hatch
www.hatchsf.com

Heather Moore/Skinny La Minx
www.skinnylaminx.com

Hemingway Design
www.hemingwaydesign.co.uk

Hybrid Design
www.hybrid-design.com

Hirschmann Design
www.hirschmanndesign.com

I.D. International Design Magazine
www.idonline.com

Identica
www.identica.co.uk

Inseq
www.inseq.net

James F. Kraus
www.artguy.com

Jenny Orel/Olga Baby
www.roteprinzessin.de

JHI
www.jhigoodidea.com

Jonathan Adler
www.jonathanadler.com

Jorge Jorge
www.jorgejorge.com

Josh Owen
www.joshowen.com

kidrobot
www.kidrobot.com

konnectDESIGN
www.konnectdesign.com

Lance Wyman
www.lancewyman.com

Lizzie Allen
www.lizzieallen.co.uk

Lorena Barrezueta
www.lorenabarrezueta.com

Lost O
www.losto.org

Lovegrove and Repucci
www.lovegroverepucci.com

Lowri Davies
www.lowridavies.com

Mark Gane
www.marthanadthemuffins.com

Mayday
www.maydaylivingbrands.com

meat and potatoes, inc.
www.meatoes.com

Merz
www.merz.co.uk

Michael Braley
www.braleydesign.com

Michael Browers
www.michaelbrowers.com

Michael Pinsky
www.michaelpinsky.com

Mini Moderns®
www.minimoderns.com

nextbigthing
www.nextbigthingcreative.com

Nicholas Felton/Megafone
www.mgfn.net

Nicholas Holbrook
nholbrook@blueyonder.co.uk

Nick White
www.thisisnickwhite.com

Old Town
www.old-town.co.uk

Out of the Blue
www.ootb-london.com

Paul Loebach
www.paulloebach.com

**People Will Always
Need Plates**
www.peoplewillalwaysneedplates.co.uk

**Philippe Starck
S+ARCKNetwork**
www.philippe-starck.com

Pieces of You
www.piecesofyou.co.uk

PhotoGenic Images Ltd
www.photogenicimages.com

productofyourenvironment
www.productofyourenvironment.co.uk

Pulpo
www.pulpo.biz

Ravi Poovaiah
www.idc.iitb.ac.in

**Reich+Petch Design
International**
www.reich-petch.com

Retired Weapons™
www.retired.jp

**Richard Steppic
available at Exclusively
Washington**
www.richardsteppic.com
www.exclusivelywashington.net

Rimmington Vian
www.rimmingtonvian.co.uk

**Robert Dawson Aesthetic
Sabotage**
www.aestheticsabotage.com

Rollout
www.rollout.ca

Sagmeister
www.sagmeister.com

**Salvartes Estudio de Diseño
y Publicidad**
www.salvartes.com

Seletti
www.seletti.com

Squires & Company
www.squirescompany.com

Studio Printworks
www.studioprintworks.com

The Art of Wallpaper
www.theartofwallpaper.com

**The Decoder Ring
Design Concern**
www.thedecoderring.com

The Polyphonic Spree
www.thepolyphonicspree.com

Tracy Dobbins
debrifield@earthlink.net

Turner Duckworth
www.turnerduckworth.com

UMS Design Studio
www.umsdesign.com

Wendy Earle
keenssoper@btinternet.com

Photography Credits
By Image Number

Early Symbols
003 Source: istockphoto.com
004 Leo Reynolds
005 Source: istockphoto.com
006 Source: istockphoto.com
008 Leo Reynolds
009 Mark Hampshire
010 Source: istockphoto.com
011 Jannie Armstrong
012 Source: istockphoto.com
013 Source: istockphoto.com
014 Mark Gane
015 Source: istockphoto.com
016–017 Mark Hampshire
018–020 Source: istockphoto.com
021 Corbis
022 Ashley Cameron
025 Keith Stephenson
026, 027, 029
Leo Reynolds
031 Mark Hampshire
033 Keith Stephenson

Membership and Identity
040 Leo Reynolds
041 Keith Stephenson
043 Leo Reynolds
044 Jannie Armstrong
047 Leo Reynolds
048 Mark Hampshire
049 Source: istockphoto.com
051 Leo Reynolds
052 Keith Stephenson
054–059 Leo Reynolds
060–068 Richard and Olga Davis
069–071 Source: istockphoto.com
072 Mark Hampshire
076–077, 081–083
Source: istockphoto.com
084, 086, 088–089 Source:
istockphoto.com
087 Gerardine Hemingway
090 Mark Hampshire
091 Ian Rippington
092–095 Mark Hampshire
097 Keith Stephenson
099 Ian Cawood
100 Source: istockphoto.com
102–103 Mark Hampshire
104 Keith Stephenson
105 Source: istockphoto.com
108 Leo Reynolds
109 Source: istockphoto.com
110 Richard Steppic
114–116 Leo Reynolds
119 and 123
Mark Hampshire
120–122, 124, 125–128 Leo Reynolds
130 and 132 Source: istockphoto.com
133 Leo Reynolds
134 Source: istockphoto.com
135 Richard and Olga Davis
137 Keith Stephenson
146 Simon Lewin
147 Keith Stephenson
153 Leo Reynolds

154 Derek Roe
155 and 160 Jannie Armstrong
156 Derek Roe
157 Leo Reynolds
161–169 Keith Stephenson
171–172, 177 Tom Austin
173–176 Richard and Olga Davis
179–181 Leo Reynolds
182 Jannie Armstrong
183 Keith Stephenson
184, 186, 189 Jannie Armstrong
185 and 187 Source: istockphoto.com
191–192 Mark Hampshire
193 NASA
201 Mark Hampshire and Keith Stephenson
202–209 Leo Reynolds

Themes and Moods
211 and 221 Source: istockphoto.com
212 Leo Reynolds
213 Keith Stephenson
214 Mark Hampshire
215 Source: istockphoto.com
218–220 Keith Stephenson
225–228 Leo Reynolds
230 Keith Stephenson
232, 234, and 235 Leo Reynolds
236 Mark Hampshire
238 Source: istockphoto.com
249–252 Mark Hampshire
255 Jannie Armstrong
256–258 Leo Reynolds
259 Keith Stephenson
262 Leo Reynolds
263 Source: istockphoto.com
264 Leo Reynolds
265 Mark Laforet
267 Jennifer Remias
268, 269, 270, 272, and 273
Leo Reynolds
271 Mark Hampshire
274–277 and 282 Keith Stephenson
286 Christi Carlton
300 and 301 Keith Stephenson
302–305 Leo Reynolds
310–314 Mark Hampshire
316–318 Leo Reynolds

320–322 Mark Hampshire
323 and 325 Jannie Armstrong
324 Leo Reynolds
327–330 Jennifer Remias
338–340 and 345
Richard and Olga Davis
341 and 343 Jennifer Remias
342 Leo Reynolds
347 Jon Warren
348 Leo Reynolds
349 Keith Stephenson
361 and 362 Leo Reynolds
363 Keith Stephenson
364 Mark Hampshire
365–378 Keith Stephenson
383 and 386 Leo Reynolds
384, 385, and 387 Keith Stephenson
389 Andy Curry
392, 394, 395, 396–398
Jennifer Remias
406 Keith Stephenson
411 Richard and Olga Davis
414–419 Mark Hampshire
420–422, 424–426 Leo Reynolds
434 and 436 Keith Stephenson
435 and 440 Leo Reynolds
437, 439, 441, and 442 Source:
istockphoto.com
438 Mécia Bento
444 and 449 Keith Stephenson
445, 448, 451–453 Leo Reynolds
450 Hilde Bakering
454 Jennifer Remias
461 Mark Hampshire
467, 468, and 469 Leo Reynolds
471–474, 476, 479, 480
Leo Reynolds
478 Keith Stephenson
486 Mark Hampshire
488, 489, and 490 Keith Stephenson
496, 498, 499, 501, and 502
Mark Hampshire
504 Keith Stephenson
505 Doerte Fitschen-Rath
511 and 512 Keith Stephenson and
Mark Hampshire

Acknowledgments

First of all, many thanks to the team at RotoVision—especially Jane Roe, Tony Seddon, and April Sankey. From our team, we thank Spike for knocking everything into shape once again.

Special thanks to Lance Wyman for writing the foreword to the book, for contributing wonderful work from a distinguished career, and for great support throughout writing the Communicating with Pattern series.

As always, we've been overwhelmed with great design contributions and our thanks (in no particular order) go to: Conrad Lambert, Nick White, Ben Newman, Michael Pinsky, Michael Braley, Turner Duckworth, Ruth at Exclusively Washington, Todd Gallopo, Anita at Rollout, Melissa at Studio Printworks, John Homs, Anna Lewis, CIRIC, and Wendy Earle.

We have been lucky to have access to the images of some amazing photographers, many from flickr.com. A special thank you to Leo Reynolds who has allowed us to source from his infinitely fascinating collection of photographs, and also to Jennifer Remias and Jannie Armstrong for fabulous shots of subjects we would never otherwise have been able to feature.